Your LIFE ON FIRE

FINDING MEANING AND PURPOSE IN A NOISY, HECTIC WORLD

*Your Life On Fire: Finding Meaning
and Purpose in a Noisy, Hectic World*

**2025 fEMPOWER Press Trade Paperback Edition
Copyright © 2025 Lianne Kim**

Published in Canada, for Global Distribution by fEMPOWER Publications
www.fempower.pub | For more information email: media@fempower.pub

ISBN trade paperback: 978-1-998721-28-3
Ebook: 978-1-998721-29-0

To order additional copies of this book: media@fempower.pub

Your LIFE ON FIRE

FINDING MEANING AND PURPOSE IN A NOISY, HECTIC WORLD

LIANNE KIM

Kristine Beese | Parastoo Boroumand | Brenda Brix | Cari Brunton | Kelly Caisse
Gloria Esguerra | Krista Frahm | Shannon Gallagher | LisaMarie Gauthier
Cristina Balau-Hodgins | Shaughnessy King | Melissa Lucas Thomas
Judi Luttieri | Danielle Paes | Crystal Samuels | Amber Skidmore
Jacqueline Smith | Erin Tee | Mikki L. Wilson

CONTENTS

INTRODUCTION

Dear Reader,

My name is Lianne Kim, and I am grateful you are here. The fact you're reading this tells me you're interested in creating a life for yourself that feels meaningful and purposeful.

First, let me tell you a little bit about myself. I've been in the coaching and mentoring space for the last decade, and over that time I have helped thousands of women design powerful and purposeful lives and vocations. As a business mentor, I help guide women to create a life on their own terms doing what they love. I have done this through my many coaching programs, my highly ranked podcast, my social media presence, my conferences and live events, and now in three best-selling books.

To say I am passionate about helping women would be an understatement. I *live* to help women. It is my mission to ensure that the women who come across my work feel seen, understood, and supported through their journey.

You might be wondering how I got here, but I won't go into too much detail about that here because a) I've shared that journey in my other books, most notably my first solo book *Building a Joyful Business* (it's a great read, if you're up for it!), and b) because this book is about YOU!

You are here because you are interested in living with more purpose and intention. You're likely curious and open to new possibilities. Or maybe you're looking for examples of women who have made bold shifts in how they approach life and work. Maybe you're at a point where you are ready to make a bigger contribution and impact on the world.

Whatever your reason for reading this, there is a good chance that you and I are not too dissimilar. I am a woman in midlife juggling career, family, and obligations. I have bills to pay, just like you. I have people who need me, just like you.

About ten years ago, I found myself in a mediocre sales job that paid the bills but didn't light me up the way other things did. It provided me with a steady paycheck, benefits, some semblance of security . . . but it was never my dream.

When I gave myself permission to dream beyond just supporting myself and later my family, I realized that I had been feeling deeply unfulfilled. I spent my days running on autopilot, as they say, rushing from home to work to home again to the daycare to pick up my kids, back home to make dinner, bath time, bedtime, sleep, then repeat the whole thing the next day. Every moment of my waking hours was accounted for, but when I really looked at where my time and energy were going, it was largely to serve other people's needs.

Making sure my kids were fed and cared for.

Making sure my husband felt loved and appreciated.

Making sure my aging parents were healthy and happy.

Making sure my friends and siblings felt supported.

Making sure my boss thought I was performing well at work.

And this was just the beginning of the list. When I really stopped to think about it, I could see that I was leaking energy because the majority of my days were filled with tasks I didn't really want to be doing.

I didn't love sales, but it's the career I fell into, and it paid well. And this feeling extended beyond just work. Everywhere I looked I could see obligation after obligation. It was taking a toll on me, mentally and physically. I could feel burnout setting in. Even my leisure activities didn't fuel me like they once did.

So, I decided I had to do something about it!

By this time, I had a small side-hustle business. I started hosting meetups in my area for female entrepreneurs, and after a few of these, I could feel the spark coming back. I would leave these events feeling excited, hopeful, and curious about what else I could do along these lines.

Soon after, I started sharing my own knowledge with these women about the kinds of things that could help them improve their lives and businesses. Some was more tactical stuff like sales and marketing, but some was more motivational as well.

Pretty soon I had women asking me questions about the kinds of things I could help them with. And not long after that I started offering my expertise in small doses in exchange for a nominal fee. This would become the beginnings of my coaching packages.

The truth is, I didn't really know what I was doing . . . but I didn't care. I could see that the knowledge I was sharing was making a difference in these women's lives and it felt amazing! With every meeting or coaching session, I felt that spark grow a little bit more. What started off as a small ember would soon grow into a steady burn until eventually one day I couldn't contain my excitement anymore.

I had just come from one of our meetups where I had shared some tips on sales and marketing. It was an area I knew well, and the group had a lot of questions. As I was speaking, I could feel them leaning in, nodding, and really soaking up every ounce of what I was sharing. To me it was just stuff I learned in my sales jobs, but to them . . . it was life changing. I knew instantly I was handing them the keys, and not only to a better and more lucrative business but to a better life!

After that event, I couldn't sleep. My mind was spinning, replaying my favorite moments over and over. I had new ideas about things

I wanted to share and ways I could help these women. Whenever I thought about it, all the hairs on my arms would stand straight on end, and I could feel the blood coursing through my body. It was a very visceral feeling, and I remember thinking, *I feel on fire!*

Shortly after, I was sitting on my sister's couch in East Toronto, bubbling over as I recounted the details of this event. She could see how palpable my energy was. I went on and on for the better part of an hour about how exciting it was to help people and how fulfilled I felt because for the first time in my adult life I felt like my work was making an impact.

I finally paused to take a breath. She smiled and said, "Lianne, this is your thing!" While I don't recall telling her that I had felt unhappy, I suppose she could sense it. After all, how I was showing up in this moment must have been a vast difference from the times she had seen me in recent years.

Looking back, I don't think I'd ever felt so alive!

The fact that I was feeling this way and one of the most important people in my life could see how special this was, really caused me to pause and take notice.

I think we all have moments like this, moments of joy and clarity that show us we are on the right track. However, we don't always appreciate how powerful these moments are. For me, I knew I wanted to pursue this path, but I had no clue how I would do that. I had a full-time job, two kids, bills to pay, people to support. How could I possibly make a living doing something like I was dreaming of?

But that didn't stop me from taking the next steps. Soon after, I was speaking regularly to women's groups and coaching a handful of clients at a time. I was doing it here and there, whenever I could fit it in. And with each passing day, another chapter would unfold. It felt as if I was attracting all the people, events, and opportunities into my life that were supposed to be there.

I still didn't know what I was doing, but I was figuring it out. I knew things would unfold as they should, so long as I kept listening to that voice inside me that said, "Keep going, you're on the right track." I didn't have to see the whole staircase, just so long as I continued to take the next step, then the next one after that, and so on.

If you're anything like me, you deeply crave making a meaningful impact on the people around you. You want to put quality work into the world, work that truly makes a difference. You want to feel satisfied knowing your talents and contributions are being utilized and appreciated.

You don't want to merely go through the motions in life. You want to live a bold life. A life of meaning and purpose. A life on fire!

But perhaps, like me, you fare better when you have access to clear examples of other women who are doing what you want to be doing. It's said that success leaves clues, but so does fulfillment. My experience has shown me that we love learning from people who have achieved the kinds of things we want to achieve because it makes success feel more tangible.

This book is a collection of heartfelt stories from twenty amazing women who are all finding meaning and purpose in their own unique ways. These authors share how they had to overcome significant challenges to get to the life they dreamed of. They also share specific steps they took on their journey to living more purposefully.

These stories are powerful, emotional, and often raw. They will make you feel, and they will make you think. In fact, you may even see yourself in one or two of these women's journeys. I invite you to explore these pages with an open mind and heart. Take what lessons are being offered, the ones that make the most sense for you right now, and see where they may lead you.

I invite you to skim through the book, in no particular order, and linger when you feel compelled to linger. There is no need to read this book from cover to cover in chronological order, though once you dive in, you likely won't want to put it down.

Feel free to come back to this book again and again as you feel called to. If you enjoy this book or find it helpful in any way, I invite you to reach out to our authors and let them know what you liked about their chapter. We have included the Instagram handles for each author so you can learn more from each of them.

And if you love the book as much as I do, it is my sincere hope that you will pass it on to those you feel may benefit from it. After all, the more people who read this book, the more lives it will impact. And what a world this would be if everyone were more connected to their greater purpose.

May these stories guide you and heal you. May they lead you to your right next step. And may they help you to live your life on fire.

Lianne

Chapter
ONE

THE JOYFUL ROAD

To my husband, Kim, for being my codriver on this wild and joyful road; to our kids, Atley, Matthew, and Ryanne, for filling it with magic; and to the women who lift me up—I'm so grateful to be on this beautiful journey with you.

BRENDA BRIX

As founder of Brenda Brix Consulting and AMR Design, Brenda leads a visionary team turning dreams into reality. After facing burnout and health challenges early on, she built a streamlined, repeatable business model that gives her space to pursue what she loves. With design projects across Western Canada and her own sustainable furniture line, she helps entrepreneurs design businesses that support the lives they want to lead. An award-winning leader, Brenda champions collaboration, abundance, and lifelong learning and is committed to empowering women in business to live abundantly by sharing the insights she's gained throughout her journey.

@brendabrixconsulting

THE TRUTH IS,
A 50/50 BALANCE
DOESN'T EXIST. . . .
WHAT WE'RE REALLY
SEEKING ISN'T BALANCE.
IT'S ALIGNMENT.

@brendabrixconsulting

Life-work balance is bullshit.

There's so much talk now about finding balance, hustling harder, working smarter. Need I go on? But what if the very idea of the goal of achieving balance is what's throwing us off?

As a successful entrepreneur with three young kids and a large extended family, I spent the better part of the last two decades trying to create that perfect 50/50 balance and feeling like a failure because of it. That image of standing on a teeter-totter, trying to keep everything perfectly stable, only gave me anxiety and sore stomach muscles. I thought I had to be everything for the business when I was also home with three little kids. In fact, my youngest was only three months old when I started my first business, but I was drowning as a stay-at-home mom and initially saw the business as an outlet.

I didn't start out as an entrepreneur to become overwhelmed but rather wanted something that would give me flexibility, would give me meaningful challenges and change people's lives. I wanted to be everything for everyone, the perfect wife always there to support my husband. The perfect mother who packed all the lunches, who was at every game and every school event. The perfect daughter and daughter-in-law and my perceived expectations I thought that entailed. And I still wanted to have time to find personal fulfillment. I wanted to hold up to the Instagram-worthy show of what I thought my life should be, but I never took the time to step off the hamster wheel to see what my family really needed. And more than that, what I really needed.

SEEKING ALIGNMENT, NOT BALANCE

The truth is, a 50/50 balance doesn't exist. It's an impossible ideology. You're not failing if some weeks you feel like a superstar at work and a mess at home, or vice versa. The scales are not broken, they were just never meant to be scales in the first place. What we're really seeking isn't balance. It's alignment.

I dreamed of being the perfect stay-at-home mom while also a successful designer and a daughter my parents could be proud of. Someone who was perfect in every aspect of life, at least viewed from the outside. But I was burning out hard and fast. Rather than flexibility at that point, what entrepreneurship gave me was more responsibility, more commitments, and more mental load than I could handle. Everything was coming to a head where I was physically and mentally unable to continue. My husband was also dealing with the same burnout, and we didn't know how to get out of this whirlwind we were in and still support our kids.

WHEN LIFE CHANGED

I can remember the exact morning it changed for me. In 2018, I found a lump in my left breast. Let me tell you, nothing makes you take stock more than facing death. Realizing that I had to build a business that would allow me to deal with life events and be there for the kids and my husband in that hard moment was overwhelming. I didn't dream of wealth or accolades, I dreamed of having peace and time to live in the moment of what was important.

My girlfriend gave me the amazing gift of a weekend to myself in the mountains, my happy place. She offered a place for me to stay and took my kids for me so I had three solid days to become mentally prepared and think about the next steps in our lives. It was on that weekend, as I was driving home, that I had the aha moment of not looking at life-work balance as a circus act on a teeter-totter but rather as driving a beautiful car on a windy road.

MY LIFE IS A CAR

The four wheels of the car are there to support you and your life and keep you steady on the road, and ultimately, you are the driver in control of your life. You have two wheels on one side that are career and ambition, and on the other side, two wheels of health and your family or personal life. You control your speed, what road you're on, and your steering wheel. You are rarely on a straight road (unless you live in the Prairies, of course!), and that's okay. Sometimes you will steer more toward your physical health and your family or personal life. And sometimes it's okay to steer more in the direction of your ambition and career. But if you only steer in one direction, you will go in circles and just make yourself carsick. Your life is a journey on a beautiful, winding, and imperfect road. You control the road you take, the speed at which you travel, and when to stop for gas and maintenance.

 YOU ARE NOT JUST THE PASSENGER IN YOUR LIFE, YOU ARE THE DAMN DRIVER.

I fully nerded out on the analogy on that three-hour drive home, thinking of clients and other extended family members as passengers in your journey, but passengers for a time only. They don't own your car, and they don't sit in the driver's seat. As the owner and the driver of the car, I have paid somebody else to build the car. I'm hiring somebody else to maintain the car with regular maintenance and make sure the engine runs smoothly. I'm ensuring I keep the gas and the fluid levels where they need to be. In other words, I'm not the be-all and end-all. I needed to ask for more help, I needed to delegate more, and I needed to build a team together to support me in building a business that allowed me to live abundantly.

LIVE ABUNDANTLY NOW

That abundance wasn't going to be a future state when the kids were older or when the business hit a certain number. That abundance was going to be now. That delegating and building a team would allow me to be fully present in my beautiful, messy, chaotic, and joyful life. The best gift I could give myself and my family was to build a business that could support the way we wanted to live rather than the business running my life.

I wanted more time with my kids where I could actually be present and not think about a client's project. Where I could take time in the mountains to recharge and be creative on a regular basis, and ultimately, where I could earn more but work less, or work in different ways that brought me joy rather than stress.

Luckily, the biopsy came back benign, and I could go back to "reality." But my reality was no longer what I wanted. I wanted to change the narrative. I used to think asking for help or hiring somebody to delegate the things I don't like to do to someone else meant I was a failure. That if I needed help, it meant I wasn't capable and therefore had failed. But that narrative, I believed, was toxic. When I did start building a team and truly invested in the right people, processes, and boundaries, everything changed. Your team is your engine. The process you built in your business is how smoothly your car runs. The boundaries are the brakes, your airbags, your lane control—everything that keeps you on the road you have chosen to be on. And remember, you can't go full speed on bald tires and no oil.

Creating a business that supports your life is not a luxury. It's a necessity. I don't want to gloss over how much work, intention, and time went into creating that, but I cannot stress enough the value of investing in yourself and a business that supports you. The real driving force of the car analogy is realizing that you can't just drive down the road without building the car first. You don't build the business first and then figure out your life. Rather, you need to reverse engineer the business to support the life you want to have. And to do that, you need to define your perfect, average, beautiful day. Not a dream day, not a vacation day, just a real-life weekday that you would love to live on repeat. What time do you wake up? What do you see when you open your eyes? What kind of conversations are you having during the day? And what does your workplace feel like?

LETTING GO OF EXPECTATIONS

The hardest part of all of this was letting go of expectations about what I thought my day should be and allowing my mind to expand to what I actually wanted it to be at this time in my life. I still had three little kids, a mortgage, and all kinds of responsibilities, but switching the mindset that I was in control was liberating. Once you know what you want out of your life and your day-to-day, you can set boundaries to build a business that gets you closer to that day every day.

SETTING BOUNDARIES

At first, the hardest part for me in setting boundaries was shifting my mindset. I needed to understand that boundaries are not about saying no but rather they are about saying yes to what really matters to me and my family on my perfect day. That saying yes to protect my time is a good thing. That saying yes to doing productive deep work that I'm good at and delegating the things I don't excel in to somebody else protects my time and my mental health. That taking weekends off and only meeting with clients during the week is okay and don't require any guilt. I don't look at boundaries as hard walls but rather as my internal compass that allows me to navigate the chaos of a young family with grace.

So, I started with small boundaries to get used to it:

- I maintain set office hours, which are listed on my website, in my agreement, and in every piece of brand communication my clients receive.

- I only check emails three times a day. I'm not a heart surgeon, and there is no true emergency in my business.

- I've defined who my ideal client is and set processes in place to be able to say no to the clients that would drain me or on projects I would not be profitable on. I've stopped saying yes to "small jobs" that took massive time and brought little joy. I've chosen to specialize in what I love and what lights me up.

- Calendar blocking has been a game changer. By having the big and small life events in my calendar, I know, and my team knows, to protect them like gold. This allows me to book vacations and to block off time for rest and creativity.

- Leveraging technology and technology experts is huge for me. I know how I want our process to work, and I hired the people who know how to set up all the software and automations to make it work. I also love how the ability to transcribe anything with my phone has opened up how and where I do business. I have unchained myself from my desk, and unless I'm meeting with a client face-to-face, I can work from anywhere. In fact, I'm "writing" this chapter as I sit on a deck in the Rocky Mountains with an amazing view, a fire, and a glass of my favorite red wine. I don't have a computer or a notebook; rather, I'm speaking into my Air Pods and it transcribes it into a Google Doc. This is also how I write all my courses for my consulting business, and I do so while I'm paddling or hiking. Tech allows me to schedule time in my happy place while doing creative work.

SELF-CARE AS MAINTENANCE

I now prioritize self-care without apology, as my energy is my greatest asset. I learned this the hard way when I had a full-circle moment when I found a large lump in my other breast in the fall of 2023 and was diagnosed with stage 2, grade 3 breast cancer. It was an amazingly hard thing to go through, but I am so thankful I had taken the time and set the intention to put up these boundaries to create the processes and build a team. I was able to take time for treatments. I was able to take time to go to Panama and give myself some mental space during the yearlong journey. And because I had processes and boundaries in place, I could step back without my business falling apart. Self-care isn't indulgent. It's essential maintenance. These boundaries are how I keep my vehicle from crashing, and when you put your life into the perspective of being a car, that's the last thing you want to do: crash. I don't even look at any of these boundaries as optional—they are an essential part of the operation.

Knowing what I want my perfect day to look like, and setting the boundaries and intentions, has allowed me to design joy into my life again. I have a colorful printout of my essentials that I hang above my computer so I see them every day that I sit at my desk and ensure they remain my top priority. I schedule a week of hiking in Canmore, Alberta, every fall, and another week in Nordegg, Alberta, every spring. I take every Christmas break and long weekend as a given. I no longer look at this time as indulgent but rather as the strategy to create the business that I need. I am just as intentional about having joy as I am about meeting deadlines, and it has become the foundation of success rather than the reward. Abundance is my daily practice.

Today, I run three successful businesses. My interior design firm, AMRDesign.ca, which is streamlined and with clients and collaborations that bring me so much joy. My consulting work with other entrepreneurs at BrendaBrix.com brings me deep fulfillment and can be done from anywhere in the world, which allows me to travel. The sustainable furniture, BrixandCo.com, is a passion project that I've had the time to put into place due to the other businesses being so streamlined with the proper support.

This year, as my kids are all now teenagers and what they need from me has changed, my perfect day has also adapted. I start my days later, making space for yoga, journaling, and silence before emails. That one shift dramatically improved my productivity and mood.

Don't wait for that crisis moment to start the process of building your car—your life—into what you want. You can live abundantly right now no matter where you are. You just need the right road map . . . and the courage to pick the road you want to be on. So, take your foot off the gas, roll down the windows, and enjoy the ride.

Chapter
TWO

LIFE IS THE BUSINESS

In loving memory of my parents, Earl "Chickie" and Florence "Sue" Wilson, thank you for being my blueprint. Your love, values, and spirit continue to guide every move I make. This work is an extension of our legacy. May the work I've done speak for us.

MIKKI L. WILSON

Mikki is a strategic connector, capacity concierge, and community builder who built her brand—The Dot Connector—before building her business. After fifteen years in marketing and business development in wealth management, she transitioned from career to caregiver to connector, then launched a consulting practice to transform her relational superpower into sustainable impact. As founder of Dot Connector Consulting and DotConnectHer, she helps women take the work out of networking and build the support systems they've always needed but rarely know how to ask for. Mikki empowers women to lead like CEOs—not just in business but in life, community, and care.

@mikconnectsdots

UNFINISHED BUSINESS DOESN'T MEAN FAILURE. . . . IT MEANS THERE'S STILL MORE OF *YOU* TO LIVE.

@mikconnectsdots

I can still hear Chickie's words ringing in my ears: "Life is the business."

His voice was sobering, in the most unexpected moment. It was May 5, 2015, and we were outside, leaning against the back of my dad's Dodge Charger. The sun was hot. The sky, cloudless. And minutes before, Flo—my mom, best friend, and biggest supporter—had just taken her last breath. I remember the way the warmth of the car met my back as the world kept moving while mine had just fallen apart. I was crying, numb, shattered. Yet, what he said next didn't shock me one bit.

"Well, Mik, you can cry for a day or two, but after that, you gotta get back to business."

Any other time, I would've brushed it off as the usual "shit my dad says." But that day, it started making sense. I knew what he meant: Don't stay stuck; keep moving forward. My entire life, this man would say: "Mikki, you've got to handle your business."

I thought he meant work. Job. College. Career. But standing there by his side, on the first day of life without Flo, I understood what he was saying. This—loss, transition, life—*was* the business. Not the degrees, the career, the titles; the business of *being* human. That one sentence unlocked the Wilson family philosophy: *Life is the business.* Not professional versus personal. Not work-life balance. But a focus on the bigger picture. So, I cried for a couple days, took care of my business, and kept it moving.

CONNECTING THE DOTS

It took two weeks to "pull it together" before I could walk back into the office. After that, work felt like the only way to move forward. I appeared to be "successful," whatever that meant, and was moving nonstop—networking, attending events, and saying yes to every opportunity. I was becoming highly visible and that turned me into a brand: The Dot Connector. The girl who gets stuff done.

But I was grieving out loud in silence.

When I flashback to Flo's funeral, I assumed it would be small—mostly family. I remember looking around the room, and it was *full*. It wasn't just the number of people but who they were that surprised me. People from every part of my life: coworkers, old classmates, community leaders, women I'd mentored, friends I hadn't seen in years. My network had shown up to support me. And what's wild is that everyone wanted to meet Chickie. I still laugh thinking about how he snapped at me: "Why do you keep bringing all these people up to me?!"

"Because, Dad . . . I'm pretty cool. And if they think I'm cool, then of course they're going to want to meet *you*."

He was not impressed.

That moment was a mirror. I felt seen and supported. I could see how much I'd invested in building a network and how interconnected my circles had become.

THE POST-IT NOTE THAT KEEPS ME GOING

A few days after the funeral, I found a handwritten note Flo had written years earlier for Valentine's Day. It read: *I am so lucky to have you for a daughter. I am so proud of you and the things in life that you have accomplished. Don't stop until you get to the top. Love, Ma.*

I keep that note close. Because when the days got dark, and they did, that note kept me going. Much like my dad, she had her own advice:

"Never settle for less and don't depend on a man."

Even though she was gone, her message was clear: Independence, especially as a woman, is important.

SEEING THE BIGGER PICTURE

Looking back, I didn't realize what I was building. My trajectory felt disconnected, like dots scattered on a page. But now, I see that every resource, every opportunity, every connection—those were the dots. The network. The bigger picture.

The truth is, people have always come to me with their problems. And if I didn't have the solution, I provided the pathway. I supported them in finding the clarity they needed to move forward. I didn't know this was a gift until my friend Lance, an instructional designer, explained it so matter-of-factly after I vented to him and asked, "Why do people always come to *me* with their problems?"

"Because you're The Dot Connector," he said.

He went on to explain how I was a node inside a network. A center of influence with social capital. People came to me because they trusted that I could help—and I delivered. It made sense. And the name had a ring to it. It also felt rooted in my identity, and at that point in my career, it was way better than being called "the marketing gal" or "the girl who makes things pretty."

I wanted a reputation that people respect. The Dot Connector wasn't a nickname, it was what I was becoming known for. It was how I built a bridge between life and business. It became the foundation for everything I was, and am, building. And it didn't take long for my reputation to precede me.

CAREER WOMAN, CAREGIVER, CONNECTOR

Nine months after Flo got her wings, I was emceeing an event when my phone wouldn't stop vibrating. A number I didn't recognize kept calling.

I silenced it. We were scrambling to set up, and I was in hustle mode—smiling, executing, running point. The night was a success.

The next morning, I slept in and hadn't checked my voicemail. It wasn't until that afternoon, when Chickie's landlord showed up on my doorstep, that the dots began to connect. He told me an ambulance had taken my dad to the hospital.

That's when I listened to the voicemails from Mass General. "Your father has suffered a massive stroke . . ." And just like that, I found myself back at the intersection of caregiving and crisis management—making decisions, signing paperwork, speaking to doctors. That night, I had to make a life-or-death decision. I called a friend for guidance. But ultimately, the call was mine to make.

It wasn't the first time I had to make critical decisions under pressure. When Flo was first diagnosed with breast cancer, I was her caregiver. We navigated her mastectomy and recovery together. When she was later diagnosed with stage 3 ovarian cancer, chemotherapy transitioned into home healthcare. I was by her side through the surgeries and her decision to shift into hospice.

Now, here I was again, back in the thick of it. No strategy. No plan. No support. Only instinct and intuition.

WORK-LIFE BALANCE IS A LIE

On the outside, I appeared to be "crushing it" in my career. I was Director of Marketing and Business Development for a small wealth management firm, and my performance was extraordinary. Yet I was constantly being reprimanded—for optics. I was trying to balance bouncing back and forth between my apartment and my dad's place, along with the new demands of caregiving, while trying to maintain this image of having it all together.

I was exhausted. Burned out. Depressed. I barely slept. I would still show up despite looking like "who did it and ran," and most days, I was crying behind closed doors. My social life was on the back burner. I had given up on relationships and friendships yet held on to this fantasy that someone could save me. But no one came. And I quickly learned that the illusion of work-life balance was a lie.

ENTREPRENEURSHIP AIN'T EASY

Flash-forward to 2018. The CEO I was working for *suggested* I take a sabbatical. Six weeks to "figure it out." My options were to either get my optics together and keep my career or go part-time, no health insurance, but keep my title.

I took the sabbatical, but the decision was clear: family first. I effectively retired from a fifteen-year career at forty to become a full-time caregiver. It lasted all of six months before I needed something else to do. I've been working since I was fourteen. And full-time caregiving? It was driving me insane. When I considered starting a business, I remember thinking: *It can't get much worse than this, right?*

By 2019, I started a business because I felt like I literally had nothing left to lose. Spoiler alert: There was more to lose. My paycheck. My passion. My purpose. But what I found on the other side of loss was a freedom I didn't even know existed!

BECOMING THE CEO OF MY LIFE

Chickie passed away in 2020. It was a blessing being with him when he transitioned, like I was for Flo. Those two days—and losing the two people I trusted most—were the hardest days of my life. After that, I took a full year off. I was completely burned out. No business. No schedule. Just a lot of time by the ocean wondering what's next.

I wanted to heal, but I didn't know what healing looked like for *me*. All I knew was that I couldn't keep pretending I was okay. So, I gave myself permission to fall apart and pull myself back together, one piece at a time.

Healing ended up looking like a lot of the things I thought I'd never do:

- Attending wellness retreats and nutrition coaching
- Crying in circles with women I barely knew
- Regulating my nervous system with hypnobreathwork
- Practicing movement and meditation
- Trusting others to hold space for me
- Learning how to trust myself, again

That year gave me enough energy to start reclaiming my life. Not as a brand. Not as a business. But as a human *being*. I promoted myself to being the CEO of my life.

ARE YOU THE CEO OF *YOUR* LIFE?

Maybe you're the woman I was just a few years ago. Smart. Capable. Showing up for everyone. But now, you're spinning in circles trying to do "all the things" with a smile on your face. People think you're thriving, but behind the scenes, it feels like you're surviving. You wish you could breathe. But you don't know how to put your oxygen mask on first and still be the woman everyone expects you to be.

I get it. But guess what? You *are* the CEO of your life. And life is the business.

You don't need permission. You need a plan. And more than anything, you need to decide that your peace, your purpose, and your profits are worth protecting. And that begins with one decision: own your CEO.

THREE STEPS FOR FINDING THE SUPPORT YOU NEED RIGHT NOW

If you're thinking, *That's too much work,* yup, been there, said that.

Here's what no one is telling you: Owning your CEO isn't about overhauling your whole life and business overnight. Trust me, I've tried that too. Ownership starts with *one* decision. *One* choice. *One* action.

So, here's a three-step strategy that shifted things for me—and it might be the framework you need right now:

1. **Identify the type of support you need.** Is it emotional, logistical, tactical, creative, financial? Be honest with yourself about what would actually help *right now.*

2. **Ask for support from the right people.** Who has shown up for you before—and who might be ready now, if you asked? Look for aligned relationships: people who offer care, clarity, capacity, not just commentary.

3. **Create a support strategy with intention.** What needs to shift in your life or work so that you're supported consistently, not only in a crisis? Support isn't just for survival, it's how you build sustainability and spaciousness.

It's not about doing more. It's about learning to lean into support.

WHAT FELT LIKE THE END WAS JUST THE BEGINNING

Looking back, everything I thought was a test is now my testimony. Every loss, every rejection, every unexpected left turn—it wasn't just happening to me. It was happening for me. I believe every "why me?" moment prepares you for what's coming next.

 LIFE TAUGHT ME HOW TO LEAD. LOSS TAUGHT ME HOW TO FEEL. BURNOUT TAUGHT ME HOW TO BREATHE. AND TRANSITION TAUGHT ME HOW TO TRUST MYSELF AGAIN.

I've written more eulogies than business plans, but those moments shaped the foundation for everything I do. Because business isn't just about money or milestones—it's the work you've done that speaks for you.

My parents weren't entrepreneurs, but they had an entrepreneurial spirit. They used to talk about taking care of *unfinished business—not* a to-do list but the parts of you that never had a voice. The truth you buried. The boundaries you never set. The dream you deferred because someone said it was too big. Unfinished business doesn't mean failure. It doesn't mean you missed your moment. It means there's still more of *you* to live.

So, who is Mikki Wilson? The Dot Connector. A daughter, a disruptor, a leader, and a trusted adviser. CEO of my life. My parents didn't leave behind a business. They left *me*. And the work they did speaks for them.

Let me leave you with some advice: You *are* the CEO of your life. Now, go take care of your business.

Chapter THREE

WHY DOES MY "PERFECT ON PAPER" LIFE NOT MAKE ME FEEL HAPPIER?

To my Sweet Alpha husband, Richard, for your loving commitment to dreaming, planning, and living our best lives full of travel, adventure, relaxation, and All Things Moxie! And to my wonderful parents, in-laws, big brother, and bonus son, for your endless supply of love and laughter!

MELISSA LUCAS THOMAS

Melissa, CEO and founder of Moxie Global Consulting, LLC and All Things Moxie Personal Development Coaching, is a visionary branding, marketing, and customer experience expert in private aviation and luxury hospitality and an executive business and personal development life mastery coach. In 2019, she launched her consulting and coaching businesses with the hope of replacing her six-figure corporate salary within two years. She hit that goal in month six! She curated her businesses to provide a lifestyle of happiness, balance, health, and wealth. A MoxieLife designed and lived on her own terms, and she coaches others to do the same!

@moxielife.melissalucasthomas

MASTERING YOUR
EMOTIONS IS LIKE HAVING
A SUPERPOWER AND
ONE OF THE KEYS
TO HAPPINESS.

@moxielife.melissalucasthomas

In 2013, I was living in my dream home with a beautiful pool in sunny Florida with my husband of five years and our beloved tiny toy poodle, Sweetpea, and I had an exciting career as a senior level manager at the world's largest private jet services company. It was all so perfect on paper, yet in quiet moments when I was alone, I felt like something was missing. I was perplexed and continuously wondering, *Why am I not happier?* An internal whisper repeated the question, but without an answer, the voice grew louder and louder, almost demanding an answer from me.

Weeks turned into months with the question on repeat in my mind, and I began to feel guilty about not feeling happier and grateful for the life I had. *What part of my life can I be happier about?* My marriage? No, I didn't think so. I loved my husband, so why would it be that thought? My work? No. I loved my work and was actually two years into my favorite role of my corporate career at the time: building a franchise concept from the ground up. Children? No. I was always surrounded by nieces and nephews and had plenty of children in my life to love, which satisfied that space. I was questioning all the external factors in my life and wasn't coming up with answers. *Am I approaching this in the best way?*

THE DOWNSIDE OF BEING A HIGH ACHIEVER

Since I was a child, I've always been a goal getter and high achiever—some might say an overachiever—who was taught to work hard, practice hard, and be a winner. The fear of losing was always my motivator, and not being the best at something was never an option, which spurred me to focus on excelling in school and in all extracurriculars, especially swimming and softball. I treasured my awards and accomplishments, but this tunnel vision meant I didn't really enjoy the activity or the competition unless I won. My twenties and thirties were a "rinse and repeat" cycle of the same goal setting, hard work, perseverance, and sheer determination forged in childhood. And it's what spurred me to achieve my goals for success that got me to the "my life looks perfect on paper" part, which I am super proud of accomplishing. But it also laid the groundwork for not feeling satisfied with the present because I was always looking ahead to the next goal to accomplish.

It was 2013 when I realized I had finally achieved the goals I had dreamed about having in my life: a successful career with a six-figure salary, a beautiful home in Florida (the state I had always wanted to move to), a wonderful husband, and an adorable dog. I was never taught to dream about my own personal wants and needs. After all, I was a leader, a doer! I was too busy achieving and pleasing others both at work and at home to ever ask myself the deeper questions like *How do I feel about myself? What lights up my soul? What do I want my legacy to be?* I was so busy working that I forgot to build a life. But it was more than that—I didn't truly know myself. I had meticulously designed my career but not my life!

BECOMING MY OWN PROJECT

I redirected all the positive qualities that helped me be successful in my career like being driven and being an overachiever toward learning about and educating myself on the topic of happiness. I consumed tons of information on my own, both in books and videos, to uncover the key to my happiness. There is great educational content widely available to anyone, and I took advantage of it. I also invested in myself by hiring not one but two different personal development coaches. Each had expertise in helping people become the best versions of themselves and overcoming challenges in life. Their philosophies and practices were completely different, and I loved them both for different reasons. Hiring a coach is something I highly recommend because I know it helped me get results significantly faster than I ever could have on my own. Conversations with trusted friends also provided valued encouragement and support.

THE POWER OF A WORD

The very first practice I learned about and implemented was a New Year's "Intention Setting." It's where I learned the difference between setting goals versus setting intentions. My coach taught me her personal philosophy and practice for choosing a word of the year. With my discovery work, "fearless" became my very first word of the year in 2013. I must share that this is not simply choosing a word of the year. It is a curated discovery process where you use a specific series of questions to reveal the most powerful word that resonates in your soul when you uncover it. The practice was so incredibly powerful in my journey toward feeling happier in my life that I have used the practice religiously every year since. At the beginning of 2025, I decided my word of the year would be "bulletproof." I recommend keeping your word where you can see it every day, from a simple handwritten note on your desk to buying or custom creating a bracelet with your word on it. This is called visualization, and professional athletes swear by it. My word of the year has gone from being about the desire to overcome something to now representing my unshakable faith that life is happening *for* me and not *to* me. Over the years, I developed my own personal coaching philosophies and practices. I started my own personal development coaching business called All Things Moxie in 2021, and it started with my favorite personal development practice, my online course called MoxieLife Word of the Year.

Little did I know that all the uncovering and discovering work I was able to complete was about to change the entire trajectory of the rest of my life! I'm not going to lie; it was at times emotional and even difficult to examine my own life with brutal honesty. I love coaching clients through this interactive discovery work, as it is so helpful to be guided because the first word you "think" is your word of the year almost never is. Asking yourself "Why do I think this is my word?" a minimum of seven times will expose deeper thoughts, feelings, and ultimately help you discover your powerful word to drive you toward greater happiness. Most importantly, it was the first step in unlocking how I could become happier in my life and start to develop the mindset and skillset to begin living my life on purpose. What is truly remarkable is that in less than a year, I felt 100 percent happier and nothing externally in my life had changed. I had the same husband, career, dog, house, etc. It was *me* who had changed!

Within months, I experienced a major emotional shift toward truly feeling happy.

 ONE OF THE MOST POWERFUL PIECES THAT HELPED ME TO UNLOCK BOTH HAPPINESS AND PEACE IN LIFE ON A DAILY BASIS WAS LEARNING TO RECOGNIZE THE ENERGIES CREATED BY BOTH PEOPLE AND SITUATIONS.

I began practicing naming the emotions that came up for me in my day-to-day and asking myself *why* they were "stealing" my energy and happiness. This was key to shifting my own happiness. I would pause to ask myself *what* story I was telling myself and *how* could I retell myself a different story that allowed me to better protect my own energy and happiness. The bully at work became increasingly less successful at stealing my energy and creating chaos in my presence. My lack of response or participation in the negativity and chaos became a model for my team and my peers. It was fascinating how I was able to increase my peace and happiness so quickly in a situation that was previously so upsetting to me. It was the concept and catalyst for striking out on my own as an entrepreneur to found my first business, Moxie Global Consulting, a luxury hospitality and private aviation consulting business. I wanted to continue doing the work I love in a curated environment that delivers profitability and removes normalized chaotic and negative energy in the workplace. I consult with many businesses to improve their profitability strategy by designing and implementing comprehensive brand, customer experience, and operational excellence systemization in their businesses. Starting my own company allowed me to create and model for my clients a company with a culture that exudes positive energy and produces profitability!

UNDERSTANDING AND MANAGING ENERGY

The most game-changing lessons on energy came from my reading the book *The Celestine Prophecy* by James Redfield. It was an easy yet profound read that helped me instantly identify, understand, and resolve for myself how to better manage a particularly difficult personality in my workplace. Understanding energy came very easily, and I was a quick study. Managing my emotional responses to negative, aggressive, or manipulative types of people or situational energy was much more challenging. In fact, it has taken years of practice to get to a place where I am able to maintain my emotional stability. I learned to both name my emotional energetic response *and* what to do to catch a descending energy in "midair" to "toss it back up" into ascending energy for myself. I used a tool from a company called Freedom Mastery that illustrates specific emotions alongside affirmations and actions to use when you are feeling that specific emotion to educate and practice how to hold on to my own peace and happiness. The average person is most familiar with emotions such as happy, sad, angry, and mad. That is very limiting and learning more is key to maintaining a powerful and happy mindset. It's like a muscle that needs to be constantly worked out so that you are ready to flex it to protect your peace and happiness at a moment's notice. It's definitely not something I think comes easily for most people, so take it slowly. It's not an exact science, but in the moments when you are successful at managing your emotions in extremely difficult situations, it feels fantastic. Mastering your emotions is like having a superpower and one of the keys to happiness.

BECOMING HAPPIER

The becoming happier work was one of the most exciting times of my life. It was like I was my own craft project. I dove headfirst into practicing new habits and using tools to learn about myself to create bigger and deeper multidimensional dreams, goals, and intentions for who I wanted to be, envisioning how I was going to get there, and making sure I fully understood how I wanted to feel about all of it.

I also literally got crafty again, learning about the practice and many ways to create a vision board. It reminded me of being a young girl proudly pasting my swimming ribbons or softball news clippings into my big paper scrapbook. My first vision board was a huge, beautifully framed corkboard adorned with visual references of what is most important to me in all areas of my life. I have been using this same board since 2013! It doesn't change all that much from one year to the next. However, I have also been creating digital vision boards on the Pinterest app as well. With those, you can see visual cues and themes about what is happening in both my work and personal lives. It is very fun to have this easy way to look at how my life has unfolded over the years as I continue to level up my life, both personally and professionally.

TAKING ACTION TOWARD HAPPINESS

This isn't everything I learned on my journey to feeling 100 percent happier in less than a year, but it certainly gives you some of the most powerful information and steps in the process and practices I learned and implemented that got me there. I learned so much about myself and who I wanted to become and began planning on how I could do it. I felt empowered and more in control of creating my own happiness. I didn't have everything all figured out, but I also didn't feel pressured to do so. Simply learning about philosophies, habits, and practices that helped others become the best versions of themselves made me believe if it worked for them it could work for me. Then, the act of taking action strengthened my mindset to know that I could and was figuring it all out.

And because it worked for me, I am confident it can work for you too. Can you imagine unlocking feeling the happiest you have ever felt in your life and it being completely within your own control to do it? I know it's wild, but it's true! It is now my mission to help women not settle for a life that is only "perfect on paper." You deserve to feel truly happy, and you hold the power to make it happen!

Chapter
FOUR

THE POWER OF
FORGIVENESS

To my husband, Nathan, whose love and support give me strength; and to my children, Adelyn and Dean, who inspire me every day to keep growing and creating. You are my greatest blessings and my why.

AMBER SKIDMORE

Amber has a master's degree in addictions counseling and is a certified prevention specialist. A daughter of alcoholics and addicts, Amber's personal experiences fuel her passion for empowering families worldwide through education about medications and drugs. She works tirelessly to prevent the devastating impact of overdoses and to break the cycles of addiction.

@serenity_steps_p&r24

HAVING A PURPOSE
TO HELP OTHERS
GIVES ME MEANING,
AND MEANING
GIVES ME A GUIDE
TO THIS WILD LIFE.

@serenity_steps_p&r24

It was the third Wednesday in January 2018, and I had gone to our first church event since moving to Cookeville, Tennessee. That night a motivational speaker and pastor by the name of Robert Madu came and gave his speech. He spoke about how God teaches us that we need to be willing to learn new things and how there is a purpose for the pain. I had an overwhelming feeling of "Okay, I get it now."

A couple months later, I enrolled for my master's degree in addictions counseling and started school that fall.

A BROKEN CHILDHOOD

One of the earliest memories I have is of being in Kosair Children's Hospital when I was about three. I remember a red light coming in from the square window of the steel door when it was "lights out." And sitting with other kids eating cereal at breakfast. I spent about three weeks there for exhibiting "behavior" not suited for a three-year-old; I had taken a razor blade to a shower curtain and set a pile of clothes on fire. At the hospital, they deduced I had been molested, and because I acted differently toward one person in particular, they guessed it was a family member.

Being the child of addicts/alcoholics comes with its own set of challenges. I don't have any good memories about my biological dad from when I was young. My parents were divorced, and I didn't see him that often. We were scheduled for weekend visits, but he didn't always show up. I do know that his favorite drink in the morning was a "screwdriver," and he always had a drink in his hand. When I was about thirteen and would visit him, I became his designated driver anytime we went somewhere because he was always too drunk to drive. I can tell you what it feels like to be abandoned, unwanted, and unloved. At one point, my dad disappeared for months on end. He finally called and was living in Florida with a whole new family. He had gotten remarried and had a stepdaughter around my age; his new wife was pregnant with my little sister.

In January 2016, my grandmother called and told me my father had overdosed. My younger sister found him in the bathroom with a fentanyl patch in his mouth. She called her other sister who, in turn, called 911. My stepmom had passed the month prior right before Christmas. I don't know if "lucky" is the right word to use, but he lived. He was on a ventilator for a week, but as soon as he was released, he went right back to the alcohol and drugs. He was also not the nicest man when he was drunk or high. Never was! There is only so much derogatory and negative things a person can say to someone before they've had enough. I'll also say that it's NEVER okay for a father to tell their child to "eff off and go to hell."

I honestly don't even have good memories about my mom until I was older and she was sober. When I smell alcohol, it takes me back to her picking me up from the babysitter's house after a night of partying. It makes my stomach churn. I remember a time when we had to eat butter sandwiches. And another time when the police showed up at our place to find my mom drunk in the bath, my baby brother in his crib, and me in the kitchen pouring her remaining beers down the drain.

When she finally attended Alcoholics Anonymous and got sober, she dedicated herself to service work helping new members. I am eternally grateful for AA and the fact that it was able to help my mom, but as a child, I still felt like I was last on her list of priorities. I used to wish I had parents like my other friends. All four years of high school, I was a part of the Color Guard (the flag girls in the band), and I can count on one hand the number of times anybody came to support me on Friday nights or at Saturday band competitions. Some of my friends had parents who came to every band event. My senior year, my boyfriend (now husband) never missed a game.

My mom never really picked the greatest of men, especially while she was drinking. But there was one who eventually became my stepdad. I remember sitting at a picnic table with him when I was around twelve, and he told me he loved me and would never leave. Over the years, he became my dad. He was the one who was there for me when my father wasn't. He treated me as if I were one of his own, and he still does today. He has also struggled with addiction over the years. He had fourteen years of sobriety before he relapsed because of chronic back pain, which caused a lot of financial and emotional upheaval for my mom . . . and for me.

FINDING SUPPORT AND STABILITY

I met my husband in 2005 at the age of seventeen, and we got married three years later. A couple months after we got married, he joined the United States Air Force. And boy, has it been a ride over the past seventeen years. We've lived overseas in Okinawa, Japan, and in about four different States. I'm pretty used to the moving around bit, as I lived in nine different places before I was fourteen. I struggled with fertility issues for *years* and was finally blessed with my children in 2014 and 2019. God definitely knew what he was doing making them five years apart.

My husband has always been my safe space. He has shown me not only what love is but what unconditional love is as well. Even through all our moves, we try to make things as easy as we can for our children and to always make sure they feel and know they are loved.

ANOTHER TEST

In the midst of finding my path and finishing my master's degree, life decided to test me one more time. July 23, 2021, is a day I will never forget. We were in the middle of a military move. We had sold our house in Tennessee, I was doing my internship, and my family was living with a friend from church who had graciously opened her home to us. When we sold our house, we had a little bit of extra money, and my husband was able to buy a motorcycle. He'd had a few in previous years and always sold them when money was tight for our family, so I felt like he deserved to finally get the one he really wanted. He ordered it online and had been waiting months for it. It was finally ready for pickup on July 21. Two nights later, he went out for a short ride to the gas station once the kids were asleep. I told him it was fine as long as he texted me when he arrived and when he was on his way home. That was the rule we agreed on regarding the motorcycle.

It was shortly before 10:00 p.m. when he left the house. I had fallen asleep and woke up with a start at 10:30. I had a text telling me he made it to the gas station, but there wasn't one after that. I was trying to calm down by telling myself that he was fine, that he was on his motorcycle, and if I called, he wouldn't answer anyway because he was riding. *He is fine, he is okay* kept circling in my head. I decided to go back to sleep. At 11:30, I received a phone call from the local emergency room, telling me my husband had been hit by a drunk driver.

The nurse assured me he was okay, but her okay was not my okay! I immediately hung up and ran to get my friend who was upstairs asleep. "I've got your kids, you go do what you need to do," she said, and I ran to my car and high-tailed it to the hospital.

I got there as he was being rolled back into his room from his CT scan. It turns out that he was hit at 10:30, the same time I'd woken up and checked my phone. He had been unconscious since the wreck, but then woke up and asked me, "Where am I? Why am I here? What did I do wrong?"

I don't see my husband cry very often, but I could tell he was scared. And the fact that he didn't remember anything wasn't helping. Throughout the next few hours, he kept asking me the same questions over and over and over again, never remembering the answers. I was so lost, scared, and angry.

The wreck shattered his right wrist, and he had to have surgery a few days later to put it back together with rods and screws. He also had some damage to a lower lumbar vertebra and had walking issues until the swelling went down. But the mental aspect of this has impacted our family more than the physical ailments. Explaining to your six-year-old why Daddy looks a bit different and why he can't play was one of the hardest conversations I've ever had to have and one I hope I never have to have again.

At the time, I had a month left in my internship and my husband knew how important those hours were. I had the weekend to process what happened, and on Monday, he encouraged me to go to work. I was in a place surrounded by addicts and drunks, people who hurt people, like the one who drove drunk and hit my husband. Work was honestly the last place I needed to be. I didn't feel like facilitating groups, and I didn't feel like being around these people. As the week progressed, my feelings got better, but life wasn't any easier for quite a while after that.

QUESTIONING PURPOSE

Having a purpose to help others gives me meaning, and meaning gives me a guide to this wild life. I don't believe the saying that God doesn't give you more than you can carry. The God I serve, My Father, would never want me to live a life of pain. I've come to realize we live in a fallen world where we are given choices (thanks, Adam and Eve), and sometimes those choices hurt others. God gives me the tools I need so I don't have to carry life alone. And in my purpose, I share my pain so that others know they aren't alone. I give compassion to people who society calls "the scum of the earth." I know that the people I work with are somebody's somebody, so I treat them as such.

In 2017, I worked in the administrative part of a women's residential house program and fell in love with all of them. I saw parts of my own mother in those women and the struggles she went through. I carry empathy and humbleness for people who struggle with addiction because it would be just as easy for me to be in their shoes. I can help others who carry a pain that only certain people feel and live with on a daily basis. I can understand these people and hopefully help pull them out of the dark depths of hell and push them to a life in the light. I have found it's when we live in the shadows, we do our most damage.

If you work in the field of addiction, it is literally a life-or-death job. It's not always easy and can be heartbreaking when you lose a client. I lost my first one in October 2023, and I will remember his name forever. I've also lost family members to this horrible disease. I fight daily for these people to know they are loved so they can have a chance at living a beautiful life.

LEARNING TO FORGIVE

I had to learn to forgive others who had hurt me plus learn to forgive myself for the choices I made due to that hurt. I had to learn about acceptance. I had to take responsibility for the present and future. I couldn't let the past hurt me or dictate who I was every day. I could no longer play the victim of my past. I had to learn that it was okay to love myself, flaws and all. And I had to learn to build my own self-worth and stop relying on others to make me happy. To extend myself some grace. I learned that my past doesn't define who I am.

 I GET TO CHOOSE WHO I WANT TO BE AND WHETHER OR NOT I CONTINUE TO ALLOW MY PAST TO CONTROL ME. ONCE I LET THE PAST GO, MY FUTURE WAS WHATEVER I WANTED TO MAKE IT.

When I started school, I learned a lot about addiction and how it affects the person. I knew about the family component because I was it; however, I didn't really know a whole lot about addiction in general. When I started learning it was a brain disease and our bodies become dependent on the substance, it brought more clarity. I became more understanding of the patterns families carry as we're raised. Understanding this brought more acceptance into who my parents were, the childhood they had endured, and who they had become. A little at a time, I started to see the "why" I had been searching for.

Today, I can tell you that I appreciate my parents a whole lot more, even if they don't know it. I understand that when they became parents, they did the best they could with what they had. We all know there's no manual that tells us how to be parents. We're sent home from the hospital with our babies, and basically, we figure it out along the way. Today, I strive to be the parent I wish I had growing up: one who is present; one who makes my children feel valued and loved. I don't get it right every day. After all, I'm not perfect. I just try to be better than I was the day before.

Chapter
FIVE

REDEFINING SUCCESS

To my Babeski, for inspiring me to live a life full of adventure. To my Cutez, for reminding me to slow down and to laugh regularly. To Sister1 and Sister3 for always encouraging me to do bold things! I'm forever grateful that each of you never stopped believing in me.

SHAUGHNESSY KING

Shaughnessy launched her virtual assistant career after maternity leave and post-COVID. Quickly becoming burned out by the demands of solo VA work, she pivoted Success by Ness into an agency designed to provide high-level administrative support for entrepreneurs. Today, she leads a team of amazing women who support clients with systems, organization, and growth. Now with the agency thriving, Shaughnessy also hosts workshops on How to Hire a VA and speaks about how to create a life of time freedom, helping business owners step out of overwhelm and into sustainable success.

@shaughnessyking

YOU HAVE TO DO UNCONVENTIONAL THINGS IN ORDER TO GROW.

@shaughnessyking

Growing up, I was always the helper. My family used to call me "Martha," a little nod to both Martha Stewart and Martha from the Bible. I was the one who organized, tidied, planned, anticipated needs, and stepped in before anyone had to ask. It was my second nature. Back then, I didn't realize that being "the helper" could be more than just a personality trait, it could be the foundation for a meaningful career. I just knew I loved helping others, and I thought that it would lead me down a traditional path.

I started my professional career as an early childhood educator. I worked primarily with infants, then eventually worked my way up to work as supervisor. When I felt I had reached the limit with helping one company, I switched to work as a childcare center director at another childcare center where I managed the staff, cared for the children, put parents' minds at ease, and ensured the entire place ran smoothly. In 2020, running the center was obviously very different. Each day was stressful: the masking, the temperature checks, the additional rules and regulations. I also found out I was pregnant during this chaos. So, when I went on maternity leave in the summer of 2020, something shifted. That time away from the intensity of the job, combined with the chaos and uncertainty of the pandemic, gave me space to think clearly. When my leave ended, I realized I didn't want to go back.

A REMOTE RESET

I knew I needed to pivot, to find a way to use my skills in a different context, to one that didn't drain me or keep me away from my family for long hours every day. Knowing that I had a lot of transferable skills as a childcare director, I started looking for remote work. I knew I could easily do administrative work as an administrative or executive assistant. But in 2021, everyone else was also looking for work online. Remote work had become the dream for so many people, and competition was fierce.

That's when I had a thought: What if I found two part-time admin roles and made them work together as full-time income? That simple idea opened up a whole new world. I stumbled upon virtual assistance, and it felt like such a natural fit. I already had the organizational skills, the people skills, the initiative. I just needed to believe that this path was possible.

So, I leaned in. I started off small, taking on subcontract work with a well-known Canadian virtual assistant agency to gain hands-on experience and build confidence. It wasn't long before I signed my first client through them, which gave me the momentum I needed to keep going. At the same time, I began quietly searching for clients of my own, searching Facebook groups, and letting people know what I was offering. I'll never forget the excitement of landing my first solo client at $17 an hour. I was over the moon. That's the moment Success by Ness truly began.

BUILDING A BUSINESS

In those early days, I was juggling a few clients by supporting them with email management, calendar coordination, and a variety of general administrative tasks. I dove headfirst into learning everything I could. I watched webinars, devoured blog posts, followed successful VAs online, and experimented with different tools and systems to see what worked best. Every new task was a chance to improve, every challenge an opportunity to grow. Slowly but surely, my confidence began to build. I started showing up more consistently, putting myself out there, and becoming more visible. And with that, demand for my services began to grow.

By the end of my first full year in business, I had built a steady, reliable roster of clients and went from making $17 per hour to charging $35 per hour. I was officially earning more than I ever had in my previous career in childcare. The financial growth was affirming, but what meant even more to me was the lifestyle it allowed. I was working from home, setting my own schedule, and most importantly, I was present with my family in a way I had never been able to be before. I could stay home with my daughter when she was unwell, take car rides around Toronto with my husband, or step outside for a walk in the middle of the day without asking for permission. I was no longer rushing out the door each morning or coming home completely exhausted.

FINDING ALIGNMENT

For the first time in my life, I felt deeply aligned, like the work I was doing made sense not just professionally, but personally. It matched my skills, supported my values of honesty and integrity, and fit my season of life. I had created something of my own, on my own terms, and it felt both empowering and sustainable. I wasn't just building a business, I was building a life that felt good from the inside out.

In 2021, my husband had a friend who had spent the entire pandemic lockdown living in Costa Rica. After hearing stories about his friend's relaxed pace of life, daily beach walks, and newfound sense of freedom, my husband came to me with a wild idea: "What if we tried living abroad too?" At first, I was hesitant. I had the ability to work remotely with my business . . . but my husband? He didn't have a remote job at all; he would need to use his savings to make this work. The idea sounded exciting in theory, but it was completely out of my comfort zone. I had never lived outside Canada, and the thought of uprooting our life (especially with a toddler) felt daunting. But there was also a part of me that was deeply curious. What would it be like to work remotely *anywhere* in the world? To trade snow for sunshine? To live a little differently than what we were used to?

Eventually, I said yes. We rented out our townhouse in Toronto and created a plan to move to Thailand for six months. We were drawn to the warm weather, low cost of living, and the promise of adventure. But due to the ever-changing COVID-19 restrictions, Thailand suddenly became inaccessible. So, with very little time to think it through, we pivoted, and within twenty-four hours, we booked a one-way flight to Cancun, Mexico. Mexico was one of the few countries that did not have severe COVID regulations. We'd been to Riviera Maya before and found some support groups online for those looking to relocate to Playa del Carmen. It all happened so fast. We landed, found a short-term rental, enrolled our daughter in a local daycare, and tried to settle into a new rhythm.

My husband threw himself into the experience: meeting new people, exploring the city, and embracing life in a new culture. But for me? In all honesty, I hated it. I was overwhelmed, lonely, and emotionally drained. This was my first time living abroad, and I underestimated how disorienting it would feel. I deeply missed my family. I struggled with the language barrier, with the unfamiliar routines, with the feeling of being completely out of place. I wanted to love it. I *tried* to love it. But I didn't. We lasted four months before making the decision to return to Canada.

Even though that first international move didn't go as planned, something inside me had shifted. The experience opened my eyes to a new way of living. I realized how much I craved freedom—not just the freedom to work from anywhere, but the freedom to choose how I spent my time. I wasn't just looking for location independence, I was longing for time independence too. The kind of lifestyle where I could be present for my family *and* be energized by meaningful work. Where my days felt spacious, not rushed. That realization stuck with me.

FINDING THE RIGHT FIT

Fast-forward to 2023 and we decided to try again, this time with more intention and a better sense of what to expect. We spent six months traveling through Southeast Asia, living in Thailand, Vietnam, and Indonesia. The pace was slower, the culture rich and beautiful, and the food unforgettable. It was exactly the kind of immersive, soul-stretching experience we'd hoped for. But logistically? It was hard. Most of my clients were based in North America, and when I broached the topic with them, they were not overly enthused with the twelve-hour time difference. This meant I had to make the decision to step back from client work to essentially take a sabbatical. Once again, my husband was also taking a sabbatical from work. I tried my best to enjoy the downtime, to lean into our travels, and to soak up this once-in-a-lifetime opportunity. But truthfully, I felt caught between wanting to be fully present with my family and constantly worrying about our finances. Watching our savings shrink day by day left me feeling anxious and unsettled. I wanted to enjoy this life we had created, but I couldn't stop thinking about everything I wasn't doing: working, saving, growing.

It wasn't until the final leg of our journey that something finally shifted once again. I began to embrace the stillness. I found peace in simple routines: going for walks, sitting in the parks, enjoying slow dinners with my husband and daughter. I realized how long it had been since I'd had that kind of time to just *be*. No clients. No calls. No deadlines. Just life. And in that stillness, I found clarity.

For the first time in years, I had space to zoom out and ask myself some big questions: *What do I actually want my business to look like? What kind of life do I want to create for my family? What kind of work energizes me?* That season of reflection gave me the clarity I didn't know I was missing.

When we returned to Canada six months later, I felt more grounded and focused than ever before. I reached out to aligned prospects and began signing on clients who truly felt like the right fit. People who respected my time, trusted my process, and shared similar values. And many of those clients are still with me today.

I had become laser focused on hitting consistent $8K months, convinced that reaching that milestone would mean I had "made it." But the reality looked very different. In my pursuit of the numbers, I found myself saying yes to clients who weren't aligned with my values, working on projects that didn't excite me, and constantly feeling like I was juggling too much. The work became draining. The joy and spark that once fueled me were gone. That level of hustle wasn't just exhausting, it was unsustainable. Deep down, I knew something had to shift.

So, I made a choice: I let go of the clients who weren't a good fit. I stopped chasing revenue and started chasing alignment.

 I REMINDED MYSELF THAT SUSTAINABLE GROWTH DOESN'T COME FROM SAYING YES TO EVERYTHING, IT COMES FROM SAYING YES TO THE *RIGHT* THINGS.

I knew there had to be a better, more fulfilling way to scale. And that meant thinking bigger than just myself. I entered the new year with a fresh intention: to grow my business to a new level, one that didn't rely solely on me being in the weeds every day.

I didn't know exactly how that would unfold. I went back and forth between two paths: Should I become a VA coach or build a VA agency? It was the incredible Mamas & Co. community that helped me gain the clarity I needed. Their support, encouragement, and real-talk feedback gave me the confidence to move forward with building an agency model.

In the spring of 2024, we returned to Mexico, this time with the intention of staying for a full year. And something just clicked. I had hired a coach to help guide me through the process of building out the agency. I wanted someone in my corner who had walked this path before, someone who could help me build it the *right* way. With their support, I brought on my first subcontractor VA and soon paired her with our next client. That moment felt like a turning point. Not only was I no longer carrying the entire workload alone, but I realized I was also creating meaningful opportunities for other women.

And that felt bigger than any income goal I had ever hit.

THE IMPORTANCE OF ENERGY AT WORK

I've always believed that the energy we bring to our work matters. If our clients are going to receive top-tier support, then the women behind the scenes need to feel valued, seen, and aligned. I wasn't just trying to match clients with VAs, I was trying to create partnerships that felt intentional and energizing on both sides. Don't get me wrong, building that kind of business hasn't been all sunshine and roses. There have been growing pains. Tough calls. Lessons learned. But through it all, I've made a continuous effort to create the best possible experience, not only for our clients but also for the incredible women who make the magic happen every day.

Over time, I realized this meant more to me than I ever could have predicted. I wasn't just building a business, I was building a community. Supporting other women, especially fellow moms who were craving flexibility and meaningful work, became one of the deepest drivers behind everything I was doing. I'm endlessly proud of the team I've built. These women are wise, thoughtful, hardworking, and truly committed to showing up for our clients with care and excellence. Together, we're redefining what success can look like. It doesn't have to mean hustle culture, burnout, or constant overextension. It can mean collaboration, mutual respect, and building a business that fits around your life, not the other way around.

Of course, building an agency hasn't come without its challenges. I've had to get really comfortable hearing "no" and trusting that the right "yes" would come along at the right time. I've had to remind myself that not every inquiry will turn into a client, and that's okay. I've had to believe in my vision even when leads went silent, prospects ghosted, or momentum felt slow. And I've had to wrestle with the weight of responsibility because being the one steering the ship means being responsible not just for your own success, but for the success of others too. That pressure can feel heavy. Some days, it still does. But what I've gained in exchange—purpose, freedom, connection, and the opportunity to make a real impact—is worth every hard moment.

Looking back now, I can see how every challenge—from the early days of the pandemic, to maternity leave, to discovering virtual assistance, to burnout and beyond—helped shape me. They forced me to slow down, reevaluate, and realign. They pushed me to stop settling for a life that just *worked* and start building one that *felt good* every day.

If I can leave you with just one piece of advice, it is this: You have to do unconventional things in order to grow.

That might mean saying yes to a scary opportunity, moving to a different country, shifting your business model, or simply giving yourself permission to want something more. But growth doesn't happen inside the comfort zone. It happens when you dare to step outside of it (even if you're scared). Even if it doesn't work out the first time. Even if people think you're crazy.

To the woman reading this who feels unfulfilled in her life or business: You're not stuck. There's another way. You don't have to live a life that just checks boxes. You can build one that lights you up, supports your family, and leaves room for rest, travel, creativity, and joy. I'm living proof that it's possible, and that it's never too late to realign.

Ask yourself: *Am I ready to make the changes now to create the successful life I truly desire?* If so, then you're ready to take the first step. Then the next. You already have everything you need to create the life you've always wanted.

Chapter SIX

YOUR GATEWAY TO TRUE FREEDOM

To my radiant daughters, Blake and Zoey—your light, love, and laughter remind me daily why I rise, why I write, and why I dream bigger. May you always know the strength of your voices, the brilliance of your light, and the boundless love that walks beside you and lives within you. You are my truest inspiration, and the legacy I will always build for.

LISAMARIE GAUTHIER

LisaMarie is a Life Mastery Consultant, Certified High Performance Coach, and passionate guide for women rising into their highest self. With certifications in Integrated Attachment Theory and a rich background in entrepreneurship, she helps women remember their inner light, reclaim their worth, and create lives rooted in soul-aligned purpose. As the founder of *Elevating You* and creator of the E.L.E.V.A.T.E. Method and *Connection or Control? How to Recognize the Difference Between Love and Leverage™*, LisaMarie weaves together science, spirit, and strategy into powerful tools for transformation. Her work honors the sacred journey of becoming—where growth is not about fixing but awakening what has always been whole.

@gauthier.lisamarie

OUR NERVOUS SYSTEMS DON'T KNOW THE DIFFERENCE BETWEEN REAL DANGER AND REMEMBERED PAIN OR PERCEIVED DANGER. THE BODY WILL REACT THE SAME WAY TO A HARSH INNER VOICE AS IT WOULD TO AN ACTUAL THREAT.

@gauthier.lisamarie

I remember standing in my kitchen, staring at the floor, tears blurring my vision, trying to breathe through the ache in my chest. The weight of betrayal sat like a stone on my soul. I wasn't just grieving what had happened, I was grieving who I had become because of it. I ignored my instincts for too long; I was doing what seemed logical, what looked responsible, what I told myself was the "right" next step. But something inside me always knew. There was a quiet gnawing I had learned to dismiss. I didn't pause to honor what felt right. I didn't listen to the whisper of my own body. Instead, I kept performing, striving, providing—calling it growth when really, it was survival.

It was a slow drip of self-abandonment. The kind that arises when you override your own needs in service of external expectations. Scolding yourself for misplacing the keys, criticizing yourself for not being enough, judging every small imperfection like it means something about your worth. Tiny self-judgments, stacked over time, form a mountain we can't breathe beneath. That's why grace in the small things matters just as much as the healing of the big ones. You've felt it too. We all have. The pull between what your mind says you should do and what your heart quietly whispers you need.

Have you ever silenced that whisper? Chosen the predictable over the aligned? Sacrificed your truth to avoid judgment—your own or someone else's? What holds us back isn't just fear, it's internalized judgment. Attachment wounds. Unforgiveness. The quiet voice that says, "The world's external expectations are more important than our internal alignment."

In motherhood, this judgment becomes even louder. We question every decision, internalize every opinion, and often confuse self-abandonment for sacrifice. Our attachment wounds don't disappear when we become adults and parents, they get amplified. Every judgment we hold, of ourselves or others, is often a symptom of deeper attachment wounds we've never been taught to recognize.

THE THREE GATES TO HOME

These are three gateways we must overcome to truly come home to ourselves: internal judgment, external judgment, and forgiveness. When you take the time to explore these parts of yourself—your internal dialogue, your relationship to judgment, and your capacity for forgiveness for yourself and others—you will walk away with not only greater awareness but also with a deeper connection to the life you are meant to live.

This work isn't always easy, but it is always worth it.

 PEACE DOESN'T ARRIVE WHEN WE FIX OURSELVES BUT WHEN WE STOP ABANDONING OURSELVES AND REMEMBER WHO WE TRULY ARE OUTSIDE OF THE SITUATIONS AND CIRCUMSTANCES THAT AROSE THROUGHOUT OUR LIVES.

That moment in the kitchen wasn't about anger. It was about clarity. A quiet reckoning that whispered, *You've been carrying too much for too long.* I had reached a crossroads: I could keep holding what was never mine, or I could begin to release it. Not for closure but because I was ready to breathe again. I was responsible. Capable. Strategic. I had done everything they said was "right." I had created a beautiful home, a growing business, and stability for my daughters. I smiled through exhaustion and gave what I didn't have, hoping it would one day be returned. Instead, I had become a shadow of myself by the quiet ache of emotional abandonment and the suffocating pressure to hold it all together.

From that point forward, I began a slow, sacred unraveling. Not a dramatic change but a deep recalibration. I started journaling. I sought guidance from mentors, coaches, and trauma-informed therapists. I rebuilt my life from a place of inner alignment instead of external obligation. One decision. One breath. One boundary at a time.

This chapter isn't about the struggle, though. It's about the breakthrough. It's about understanding that forgiveness—of yourself and of others—is not weakness. It is neuroplasticity, your brain's ability to rewire itself. It is quantum healing, when your inner shift begins to transform your outer world. It is the act of stepping out of the familiar chemical identity of pain and choosing, again and again, to align with who you are becoming. Not who or what you've been hurt by.

Forgiveness is not about forgetting. It's about reclaiming yourself. It's about allowing the nervous system to unlearn survival and finally remember peace. This is how we begin to love ourselves so fiercely that when others see us, they know exactly how it should be done.

INTERNAL JUDGMENT: THE FIRST GATE

Have you ever felt like your inner voice was less of a guide and more of a critic? There have been mornings when I moved through the motions of motherhood: packing lunches, dressing children, scheduling meetings, all with a smile on my face and a storm inside my mind. Not because anything was wrong on the surface but because the voice inside whispered that I was already failing. Not doing enough. Not being enough.

I used to wake up with an immediate to-do list and a tightness in my chest before the world even asked anything of me. The pressure came from inside: the voice that whispered, *You're behind. You should be doing more. Why aren't you further along?* That voice wasn't even mine, not originally. It was the voice of societal and generational conditioning.

Of early experiences that taught me acceptance had to be earned. That worth was always one achievement away. That peace was something you bought through perfection and reaching the finish line. A finish line that is always changing. Sometimes it sounded like a caregiver, teacher, or someone else's highlight reel. But always, it was laced with the belief that who I was, as I was, could not possibly be enough.

If I can impart one thing, it is this: Our nervous systems don't know the difference between real danger and remembered pain or perceived danger. The body will react the same way to a harsh inner voice as it would to an actual threat. And so, we start every day in defense mode—bracing, performing, surviving—until we relearn safety, security, authenticity. We are unaware that we internalize voices before we even know we have a choice. We memorize patterns that were never meant to be permanent. Take a moment and reflect on your inner voice as you go about your day. Would the things you say to yourself be the things you would say to someone you love, or a stranger on the street?

These voices don't dissolve through logic. They dissolve through awareness, repetition, and reparenting the parts of us still waiting for unconditional love. What have you been telling yourself lately, and where do you think that voice began? Have you ever paused mid-thought and asked: Whose voice is this? Where did I first hear it? What would happen if I stopped believing it?

The first giveaway to a life you love is being aware of internal judgment. When we begin to observe, not absorb, our inner dialogue, we unlock the power to choose again. Every thought we intercept with compassion is one less pattern we pass on. Every pause is a new possibility. And in that space between reaction and awareness, we find the birthplace of freedom. Not just for ourselves but for our children who are always watching what self-love looks like in real life.

EXTERNAL JUDGMENT: THE SECOND GATE

Have you ever felt yourself shrink under the weight of someone else's opinion, especially from someone close to you? It's a quiet erosion. Not a single moment of betrayal but the accumulation of subtle comments, loaded questions, and unspoken expectations. Those closest to us often cut the deepest. Not from cruelty but from projection, misunderstanding, or unhealed pain. When you become a mother, the volume of judgment doesn't just rise, it surrounds you. Suddenly everyone has an opinion: about how you feed, parent, work, and rest. You become public domain, and your choices feel like a referendum. And the hardest part? Much of it comes from your own circle. It's not always harsh. Often, it's quiet. A comment at a family gathering. A raised eyebrow. A story shared that subtly implies you're doing it wrong. And then you begin to question yourself . . . not because you don't trust your instincts but because you're wired to want to belong.

Who are you surrounded by, and what version of yourself do they reflect back to you? Are the people in your life lighting you up or dimming your light? Are the conversations in your circles expanding your joy or subtly shrinking your spirit, the need to perform taking precedence over the ability to show up, share, and grow? Sometimes we unknowingly allow dialogue into our day-to-day lives that chips away at our radiance. Not out of malice but out of familiarity. Many of the people we keep close are yearning for the same thing—light, depth, truth—but no one knows how to name it.

Who are the people you most often talk to and how do you feel after those conversations? Expanded or contracted? Seen or small? External judgment is often quiet. Subtle. And still, it matters. What are you afraid they'll say about you? That you're too much? Too sensitive? Not doing enough? Not getting it right? When we give external opinions more authority than our inner truth, we begin to shape-shift. We dim. We people-please. We trade authenticity for approval, quietly, incrementally, until we barely recognize ourselves.

> **"Care about what other people think
> and you will always be their prisoner."**
>
> **–Lao Tzu**

Who have you been trying to prove yourself to and how has that shaped your choices or silenced your truth? What does your heart know to be true about you, even when the world doesn't see it?

The second gateway to freedom is releasing the hold that others' perceptions have on your truth. You are allowed to rise and live freely without narrating your life for those who will never applaud your growth. When we reclaim our truth from the hands of others, we model a new legacy. For ourselves and for those who watch us rise.

FORGIVENESS: THE FINAL GATE

Forgiveness is the final and often most misunderstood threshold. We think forgiveness is something we give others. But the truth is, forgiveness is a gift we first give to ourselves. Not to excuse the harm. Not to invite it back. But to stop reliving it in our own body. Have you ever carried the weight of a wound so long, you began to believe it is just part of who you are? For a long time, I did. Some days I thought I'd moved on . . . until a ringtone echoed and my stomach dropped, like I was still waiting for the next apology that would never come. I was living in a body that constantly rehearsed the betrayal. My mind was awake, but my nervous system was trapped in a loop. According to neuroscience, the body doesn't know the difference between past pain and present threat. When we repeatedly revisit a story of pain without resolution, we reinforce that emotional state and it becomes a subconscious lens through which we experience the world. Every unresolved hurt we rehearse becomes a pattern. A chemical signature that shapes how we feel, think, act, and connect.

Forgiveness interrupts that pattern. It doesn't erase the story, it changes our relationship to it. It allows us to reclaim energy that's been stuck in the past and use it to create a future. Forgiveness is not a linear process. It happens in layers. Sometimes you'll think you're done and then another layer rises. That's not failure. That's healing.

What pain have you carried so long it became part of your identity? What might life feel like without it? Forgiveness is not about forgetting. It's about choosing to no longer live from that memory. It's not about letting someone off the hook, it's about unhooking yourself from the energy of resentment. You can forgive and still have boundaries. You can forgive and still walk away. You can forgive and still protect your peace. Remember the old adage: Holding onto anger is like drinking poison and expecting the other person to die.

The third gateway to a life you love is forgiving what hurt you without abandoning what healed you. Forgiveness is the ultimate self-return. It's the moment you begin breathing in your own rhythm again, not theirs. The moment your nervous system starts trusting you to keep it safe. And once you begin to let go, not just mentally but somatically, you create space. And in that space, something surprising can arrive: abundance. Where in your life have you confused holding on with being strong? What becomes possible when you let go?

WHERE HEALING BECOMES HOME

These three gateways—internal judgment, external judgment, and forgiveness—are not checkboxes. They are living practices. Portals to the version of you who doesn't just survive but thrives. When you release judgment and unlearn attachment rooted in fear, you make space for abundance. Not just in money or success but in ease, in peace, in joy. You stop performing your life and you begin to live it. Your nervous system begins to understand that safety and joy can coexist. That you don't have to earn abundance through suffering. Abundance becomes possible when we loosen the grip of old attachments—those silent contracts that said we must prove our worth to be loved.

What would shift if I believed abundance flows not from effort but from alignment? You are not behind. You are not too much. You are not broken. You are remembering. You are choosing. You are home.

COMING HOME TO YOURSELF

When we release internal judgment, we reclaim our worth. When we release external judgment, we reclaim our voice. When we practice forgiveness, we reclaim our peace. These three gateways are not steps to be completed but pathways we return to, again and again, as we meet each new chapter of our lives. You will be misunderstood by people who haven't done their own healing. Some will judge you. Life will test you. But you are not here to live a muted life. You are here to live wide open. Loved. Rooted. Free. You are here to break the cycles that told you love must be earned through perfection. You are here to unlearn the stories that kept you small, scared, or silent. You are here to model a new way for the next generation, not by being flawless but by being whole.

So, let this chapter not be an end but an invitation. An invitation to notice when the voice of judgment shows up, and to meet it with compassion. An invitation to notice when you seek validation outside yourself, and to turn inward instead. An invitation to notice when resentment lingers, and to loosen your grip, one breath at a time. This work is not about becoming someone new. It's about coming home to the truth of who you've always been.

What would it look like to live as if you already belong? What boundaries, beliefs, or burdens would you release?

You are already enough. You are already free. Every time we choose wholeness over perfection, we quietly teach our children that peace is not earned—it's remembered. And every time you return to yourself, the world becomes a little more healed too.

Chapter
SEVEN

FALLING, LEARNING, FLYING

To Peter, whose unwavering support enables me to do this work. You have a knack for turning ideas into something real and making the impossible possible. To Daniel, Thomas, and James, who remind me every day that dreams are worth chasing and ideas worth pursuing. And to Kari and Tom, whose foundation and inspiration showed me that with hard work and imagination, anything is possible.

KRISTINE BEESE

Kristine's journey started on the national stage as an elite athlete, then it shifted to the precision world of engineering. While there, she felt stuck by the question: Why can't I get the answers I need about my money? She became determined to find those answers. From the intensity of the trading floor through the depths of a stock analyst's desk, to investing professionally, she immersed herself in the financial industry. Now, she's turning that expertise into a mission—helping women finally understand money the way she wished she could have learned years ago.

@untanglemoney

FINANCIAL PLANNING ISN'T JUST MATH, IT'S EMOTIONAL AND BEHAVIORAL. MONEY NEEDS TO SUPPORT OUR EMOTIONAL NEEDS AS WELL AS OUR FINANCIAL NEEDS.

@untanglemoney

I sometimes think of my life as a series of throws—literally and figuratively. When I was a competitive pairs figure skater, my partner would launch me into the air with all his might. I'd spin once, twice, three times . . . and fall in a spectacular fashion. Over and over again.

Until one day, I stuck the landing. I heard it takes a thousand failures to learn a new skating element. It takes a certain person and a certain mindset to throw themselves into certain failure, changing a small variable in hopes that this is the time that all the variables coalesce into a success.

A SKATER'S MINDSET IN MALE-DOMINATED SPACES

As a student, I studied engineering physics, and a company called Nortel would hire our entire class. When it went bankrupt the year before I graduated, I needed to find a different path. A friend helped me get a job in the oil and gas industry. I was the first junior engineer in a consultancy filled with seasoned experts.

During that time, I earned a lot of money. I had grit, a problem-solving lens, and a drive that shaped me. But I had no idea what to do with the money I was earning, or how to use that money to set myself up for success. Later, I would learn that I was not alone: incredibly, nine out of ten women in Canada want help with their finances.

My first encounter with the finance industry left me wanting. I walked into a local bank seeking financial advice and clarity. Instead,

I was judged for spending money on a manicure, my questions were left unanswered, and I felt like I was receiving a sales pitch for products I didn't understand. It wasn't just an infuriating interaction, it was a missed opportunity to get me to invest.

I have an assortment of insecurities, but my ability to understand concepts is not one of them. That moment lit a fire inside me. If no one would explain my money clearly and respectfully to me, then I was determined to figure it out for myself.

FROM CURIOSITY TO CLARITY

I dove into financial education and read voraciously, starting with Berkshire Hathaway's Letter to Shareholders, Warren Buffett's investment thesis.

I went back to school for an MBA, meeting the likes of Warren Buffett (a tremendous highlight), and then I joined the trading floor at RBC Capital Markets. A trading floor is a surreal place but a great place to learn a lot about money and investments. It's also a huge space, and RBC's is the largest in Canada. It consists of a variety of different business lines, all fighting for capital, with massive amounts of money trading hands and all happening in real time.

It was also a deeply sexist environment. Running jokes about rapists, boobs, and a consistent foundation of women being valued for their appearance and as objects to be acquired made it a difficult work environment. I did, however, leave knowing how inflation works its way into bond prices, and the margins the bank relies upon to make a business. The smaller the client, the larger the margin (which is the opposite of economies of scale or volume discounts).

I moved into Equity Research in RBC's London UK offices. It was my job to follow stocks of seven of the largest international oil and gas companies. It was this role that taught me how complicated it is to truly know the ins and outs of a company. I learned how to read an annual report, learned that the most important disclosures are buried in the notes, and learned that there can be risk that comes along with a corporate culture.

During my time at the bank, I watched brilliant women go on maternity leave and come back to the firm. They were normally coming off "grade A" situations (great team, great clients, rising stars within the organization), but they returned to "grade C" situations. When it was my turn to go on maternity leave, I was leaving as someone who was a favorite among investment customers because of my insights into the industry from my engineering background, and who was consistently putting out great research papers. When I came back, I was put onto a completely different portfolio within a different industry. It felt like it would take at least two years to scrape my way back to the position I was in before I went on leave, and now I had a one-year-old at home. The job required extremely long hours when I was an expert, and the hours required to get up to speed in a new industry were nearly insurmountable.

I left the firm after a short period of time and found a new role in the private equity space. There, I learned so many facets of the finance and investment industry and I now felt completely comfortable investing my money. I had a good understanding of what worked and what to watch out for as well.

I continued to take different roles in the finance industry. At one point, I worked at an investment firm where I brought in clients and helped to manage their money.

In my career, I faced yet another gendered experience. Shortly after disclosing one of my pregnancies to one of my employers, I was dismissed from the firm. These experiences cemented the connection between my gender and my financial experiences. And seeing women being overlooked, ignored, and underrepresented, married with the research showing this to be systemically entrenched in modern workforces, leads to the conclusion that women have dramatically different financial experiences than men.

THE SPARK OF UNTANGLE MONEY

My "aha" moment took shape after a conversation with a friend who confided that her relationship was on the rocks and she wasn't sure if she could afford to leave her partner. She didn't have a financial plan (and those cost several thousand dollars to create), and she didn't know what to do about her money. Could I help her? Of course, but how?

As that question rattled around in my head, others joined it. Why are financial plans so expensive? Why do so many women want help with their money? Why isn't the industry helping them? And why do women so often face disempowering pressure rather than empowering guidance?

Feeling the pull of entrepreneurship, I went to my first hackathon (a place where entrepreneurs get together and come up with creative solutions to problems). There, I met a brilliant consultant who was much younger than I am. She, too, looked to the bank for help with her money and felt dismissed by the financial industry. Our shared experiences and combined skills fueled us to develop the first, simplest version of Untangle Money: a calculator for everyday women. Women with jobs, who might have caregiving responsibilities, who might experience gaps in their career, and who have emotional needs around money.

While we were looking for investments, the venture capitalists kept asking us why we had focused on women. They weren't satisfied with our qualitative assessments, and they demanded data. And we found it. Not only did the data support the need for a financial plan designed for women but the data was also terrifying.

A single figure haunted me: In 2020, for every dollar men held in net wealth, women had only thirty-two cents (this had declined from 2010, when for every dollar men held in net wealth, women had only thirty-six cents—meaning women had lost more than 10 percent of their relative wealth in a decade). That statistic, and the persistence of the gender pay gap, the pink tax, and the growth of the gender wealth gap, made me realize that women's needs weren't an abstraction. Women are structurally underserved by financial systems. This structural disadvantage is quantitative as well as qualitative. It comes from algorithms that assume male career trajectories and the income that comes along with it, uninterrupted income flows, and no glass ceilings.

Most financial plans simply aren't built for women's lives. Worse, a woman could pay for a financial plan, follow it for as long as possible, and because her earnings won't keep pace with what an equivalent male employee will experience, she will not be able to keep up with the plan, and she'll be left feeling like she was at fault for not being able to produce the retirement laid out in the plan. She would never realize that it was setting her up for failure in the first place.

As I looked closer at the structural issues within the financial services industry, I saw increasingly more issues that were concerning. It wasn't built for people who were just starting to save and invest money.

DESIGNING FOR WOMEN'S FINANCIAL REALITIES

Untangle Money launched with a mission: get a financial plan into the hands of every woman in the world, starting with one million women in Canada. This was about creating a change in the financial confidence and understanding of most women in Canada. It wasn't just about wealth accumulation, it was about clarity, agency, and emotional confidence.

We structured our approach in a manner that didn't judge spending as frivolous (a universal complaint we hear from women) but rather focused on helping women align day-to-day money decisions ("NOW money") with their future goals ("FUTURE money"), while walking the users step by step through the process to ensure they understood each step.

Crucially, we learned that emotional needs must be treated with equal weight as numerical guardrails. Financial planning isn't just math, it's emotional and behavioral. Money needs to support our emotional needs as well as our financial needs. We needed to present the options to them in a balanced manner and let the client choose the option that would work best for them.

One thing we love to share with our networks is that women are great with money. Research shows that women are better at investing and at saving than their male counterparts. However, one area where women could improve is that women often hold excessive cash because they believe they need it for security. But new research shows that holding on to too much cash without having it invested can be a failing strategy in the long run. Because of this, we encourage women to look at a smaller amount of money to serve as a cash buffer, which is based on research, and from there, define what amount lets them sleep at night, and build around that.

Another insight: the way men's spending is socially coded as "discerning" and women's as "frivolous" skews judgment. A guy buying a single malt is praised; a gal buying lipstick is criticized, even though spending on appearance can boost women's earning potential. To combat that, we translate expenses into "hours worked." If your Flex Money is $5/hour, and that lipstick costs $40, is it worth eight hours of work? It reframes the judgment.

We also incorporated potential life stages (childbearing, caregiving, part-time work moments, and career stagnation). Our model conservatively assumes your salary will only rise with inflation. This accounts for future peaks, valleys, and gaps and enables us to map strategies that are realistic, personalized, and holistic.

THE GRIT OF BUILDING

Untangle Money's launch wasn't overnight. It's been four years of grinding: building calculators, running pilots, talking to women, refining tools. I balanced three kids at home, aged two, four, and six, when we formed the company. And I failed so many times. The words of my coaches kept coming back to me: "It's not about failing, it's about how quickly you get up and try again."

One of our first failures was during our pilot. We had thirteen women signed up to get help from Untangle Money. At that point, I thought that I could follow the FP Canada steps that Certified Financial Planners follow. Once they identified their financial goal, I built financial plans for them. Unfortunately, this is when I learned why financial plans aren't normally sold to everyday people. None of the women could afford to retire, let alone have a financial goal. It was the worst feeling in the world. I had asked the women to birth a goal, and now I was killing their dreams.

So, we decided to approach it differently. Here's where the process forced me to use some of the skills I've been honing and developing my entire life, not just as an athlete, student, or professional, but as a mom, partner, and holistic person.

Engineering skills: I knew what information we had, what information we wanted to present, and what constraints women faced. Starting with first principles (what we knew to be true), we iteratively redesigned the financial planning process from the ground up.

Pivoting: Taking what you know isn't working, finding the parts that make sense, and changing to try and solve a problem. Instead of going through a prioritization exercise by laying out goals, we decided to work through a trade-off exercise. That means we make a bunch of assumptions on your behalf and give you a starting point. We want you to react to that starting point and decide, with our support, what you're willing and able to change. This is the process that worked for hundreds of women with whom we worked.

Rooting in values: We show you other non-obvious changes you can make both now and in the future, and we let you decide which changes work for you and your situation. By working through the different permutations, you not only learn about the important concepts in finance and how they apply to your financial situation, but you also build your own financial plan that accounts for your numbers and your emotions.

Generosity and connection: The most rewarding part of the financial plan redesign process was the one-on-one moments that occurred on a Zoom call, when a woman teared up and said, "Now I get it. This is transformational. I feel seen. I feel capable." That moment was the alchemy we were looking for. Not headlines or fancy features, but lives changed. That's far more powerful than any overnight success.

Staying optimistic even in pessimistic moments: Support came sometimes when least expected. Investors approached us, inspired by our thesis that women-centered financial planning isn't a niche but necessary. Some incredible women angel investors wanted in. We were recognized by an international award for Money Awareness and Inclusion. And we also received a coveted innovation grant from the government. We used these funds to create the technology to support a self-service online product we named the Untangle MINI.

PURPOSE FOUND

Looking back, I see the arc: a skater trying, failing, learning, trying again and tasting unlikely success; an engineer solving problems using foundational first principles; a finance insider watching systems sideline women and discounting their needs; and now, an entrepreneur channeling curiosity, frustration, and empathy into empowerment.

 PURPOSE WASN'T AN EPIPHANY; IT EMERGED OVER TIME, FROM MISALIGNMENT TOWARD MEANING.

It was a voice that said, "You don't need permission. Your experience matters. Let's change the design. Make it work for the people ignored by the industry."

Purpose isn't about impressing others. It's about answering your own silent question: "Does this matter to me?" And when the answer is yes, when you feel that fire, you build, you stand, you fly.

Chapter EIGHT

PLANT THE SEEDS FOR A DREAM LIFE

To my husband, Derrick, for your unwavering support and love for me, your wild woman; to our kids, Preston and Sam, for inspiring me to continue pushing forward and making a nontraditional life pathway possible; for my parents and brother Greg, who always loved and supported me in any direction I took!

KELLY CAISSE

Kelly is a proud mother of two boys, a first-generation farmer, a Returned Peace Corps Volunteer in Africa, and a University of Connecticut graduate. She got married and started KDCROP FARMS in 2006 as a vegetable, fruit, and egg farm using organic techniques in Chaplin, CT, USA. Kelly also produces a line of value-added shelf-stable relishes, pickles, jams, chutney, and salsas that are handmade and naturally grown for the garden-fresh, farm-to-table experience. She is making it the farm's mission to teach all who want to learn homesteading and canning by providing lessons, consulting, and kits.

@kdcropfarms

CONFIDENCE IS THE KEY
TO ENTER THE UNKNOWN.
IF IT FEELS SCARY,
THAT MIGHT BE A GOOD
THING. IT PROBABLY MEANS
YOU ARE BREAKING AWAY
FROM AN OLD LIFE THAT
ISN'T AS SATISFYING.

@kdcropfarms

I would love to tell you all the steps needed to become a successful business owner, but sometimes the steps are not so clear. It's the experiences and the life lessons that lead you to finding your real superpower and niche in life.

Like most girls in the 1980s, it was drilled into my head (by parents, teachers, and society in general) to follow the straight and narrow path. Study hard, do well in school, and choose a suitable career that will accommodate a family. But that path doesn't always bring happiness or success. Sometimes the answer is found off the beaten path, in the tall grass or the tilled soil. The secret is listening to your inner voice when it says, *This is not where I want to be.*

I grew up in the suburbs of Chicago. My mother was a stay-at-home mom and made sure everything was provided and in order, while my father worked a nine-to-five job but was home for us on the weekends. Mom was an artist and brought creativity into my life. There were always new crafts she was working on. When I was a child, we lived in three different states because of my dad's job as a computer engineer. My younger brother and I learned at an early age how to start a new life somewhere over again. From Illinois to Texas to Connecticut, the one constant that made each house feel like home was the garden my dad always planted in our backyard. He found joy and pride when he harvested those delicious summer tomatoes, peppers, cucumbers, and more. And we loved eating them, and his homemade chili!

It's probably not a coincidence that my favorite childhood coloring book was about two families who met at the local fair. One family, who farmed, brought their pickles to sell, and the other family, who made pottery, brought their creations. After each family sold everything, they took their kids for ice cream and rides on the merry-go-round. It seemed like such a simple, happy life.

THE BEATEN PATH

After high school, I set my sights on pre-med. My family was so proud that I was on the respectable path to becoming a doctor, but a D in university biology quickly derailed that plan. So, I pivoted to science and excelled in a plant science lab job, counting nematodes under a microscope that were attacking corn crops in Southern Illinois. It was also my first taste of big farming and how the lab results can help farmers. This intrigued me and probably instilled in me my interest in lab work. I also loved the freedom to go into the lab whenever I wanted to do my work and get paid. I eventually switched majors to animal science but still continued working in labs.

WAY OFF THAT BEATEN PATH

In my senior year, I attended a Peace Corps presentation that changed my life. It was so far from the path I'd envisioned for my future. I actually applied without telling my parents. I graduated from the university in May with a BS in animal science, got my acceptance letter from the Peace Corps in June (and finally told my very shocked parents, who eventually supported me), then flew to Africa for a job in Tanzania that August.

My Peace Corps stay in Tanzania, East Africa, grounded me and made me realize how much I loved nature and family. It's the best job I've ever had! I was basically the town veterinarian and did all sorts of projects with the women, farmers, teachers, and children. The village loved me, and I loved them. I learned how people self-sustained their families just through farming. Seeing how the children grew up alongside their parents working next to them in the fields had me in awe. They made baskets and crafts and brought the harvest to town on bicycles so they could buy what they needed to run their household or travel to see other families. It was slow-paced, straightforward living. They had to supply their basic needs like getting water for the day, cooking their food for the day over a fire, and tending to their business/farm. Some went on to become teachers, while others got government jobs and left the village. But most were generations upon generations of family, living and farming together. They were not chained to a desk for a corporation or inside a factory. Sure, it was a hard life, but no one told you when to work and took you away from your family for a nine-to-five job. The family and the business were one. Babies were wrapped tight on the backs of the mamas as they worked the fields. The husbands worked with them, loading up for market or breaking new ground with a team of oxen. It was so beautiful, so pure, so straightforward, and I wanted it! How could I adapt this slow-paced life of Africa to our fast-paced life in America? This is where I felt the strength of the soil for the first time— the way time stands still when you are out in the field with nature.

I like to say it was nature that saved my soul and my mind! It was by candlelight that I started drawing out my plans for when I got back home. I wanted to have a farm and a nature center. It was a hard decision to leave Tanzania after my second year, but I felt I had given all the knowledge I had to them and now I had to pursue my new blueprint. My future in America was calling me back!

BACK HOME AND FINDING FOCUS

I got home and faced culture shock, then began adapting to our fast-paced life. Even driving cars seemed alien to me. I realized I had to do more research and preparation before I could make my farm dream happen. I needed to keep volunteering, so the first thing I did was apply to get EMT basic training, which planted me as a volunteer EMT. Then I worked with kids at a nature summer camp, followed by volunteering at a nature center. Next, I surprised myself by deciding to get a job at my old university under a professor doing farm-based research. This is when I decided to work with dairy farmers and vegetable growers as a consultant. I tested their soils and gathered cornstalks to be analyzed at the lab with the ultimate goal of providing fertilizer and compost recommendations. But after four years of being a lab rat with minimal time on the farms, I became extremely unhappy working for a professor who did not respect me and treated me as an underling. I was tired and mentally drained. The veil of depression had started draping over my dreams for the future. I was tired of seeing all kinds of wonderful farms and holding myself back from starting my own.

At this point, I was really at my unhappiest time. I had just put my cat of almost fifteen years down, and I decided to skip the exam for one of the graduate courses I was taking. I was sick of my job in the lab and felt like I had no future. The only bright spot was the part-time job I had started at a cheese farm. Soon after, however, I met Derrick. Within the first month of dating, I told him about my dreams and that if he wanted to be with me, he had to be part of them. He was excited about my ideas too. For the first six months, we worked together on an organic vegetable farm and at a greenhouse and learned farming techniques. Then he proposed around Christmas, and a year later we were married and decided to start our farm venture on a one-acre lot our landlord let us use. I very clearly remember the day we decided to tell my father about our idea. In shock, he said, "You will starve; there's no future in farming."

It didn't hold us back. It actually gave me a push to prove him wrong! So, I quit the university lab job, stayed with the cheese farm, and dedicated all my extra time to working on the land with Derrick. With me as the owner, we hit the ground running. It was the best first season ever on that one-acre field. Even though we found deer had eaten all the tops of the habanero plants, we still managed to harvest enough to create our first spicy jelly. We went to farmers' markets and started making pickles and jam. We loved life, and it was passing at a quick pace. We moved into our own home and were soon expecting our first child.

Being a first-generation farmer and now a mother, things were not as easy as I had anticipated. But I married a strong man who supported me in every way. We were a team bringing our newborn boy with us to market. It wasn't without its challenges, though. When our son turned two and I was working at a dairy farm, a cow kicked my arm and broke it. So, that summer I was farming with a cast and keeping up with a toddler. Carrying flats of plants and changing diapers with one hand was tricky. Then baby number two came along in 2011. By then, my husband's back began deteriorating, and he could not work the farm like he used to. By 2015, I took on all the markets and continued with my side jobs, and Derrick remained dedicated to running and maintaining equipment plus working his side job.

GOING ALL IN

In 2020, I went all in. Farming seemed to be the most important thing to us, as my side job with extension services became unstable. I felt needed and necessary as a farmer. We had so many people coming to the farmers' markets and joining our weekly veggie bag pickup, also known as Community Supported Agriculture or CSA. I felt secure in my choice and relished in being present at my home with my family.

The farm business was finally taking shape once I could really invest all my energy into it. It was also the beginning of the social media boom and the availability of online classes to perpetuate your business and strategy. It took so many years to get this far, and I felt confident that farming might be the only work I'd need to do. It was my customers who made me realize that I did make a difference in this world, one life at a time. I was humbled and thankful. It was gratifying knowing that I was truly my own boss. I could shape my business to tailor to my goals and become successful.

INNOVATION AND GROWTH

It's been a roller-coaster ride, to say the least! Today, I have so many avenues of revenue generation that I can make money under any circumstance. Every season, I come up with new and innovative ideas that keep the business afloat. Since 2023, shortly after my father's passing—which actually inspired me to pursue the next stage of my business—I have been on a mission to bring the educational part of farming to the community. From teaching at the library about starting your garden to teaching pre-kindergarteners how to plant potatoes on a field trip to our farm, I was doing a handful of in-person workshops. It seems that with rising pricing and food recalls, now more than ever people want to learn how to grow and preserve their own food. It's time to bring out the old canning jar books and instill confidence in people who don't know how to garden and preserve, showing them that anyone can do it.

What good is my time on earth if I can't pass down knowledge to people who don't know how to grow their own food or provide without a grocery store? I recalled my grammy who taught me the old ways of gardening and providing fresh meals for the family all year round, and my dad with his gardens that provided fresh vegetables for the summer. The mission of my business became clear: pass on the knowledge to all willing to learn. Now, I have pickle kits and pickle pouches available for purchase, which include access to easy step-by-step instructions that take you through the whole process of making one jar of pickles. The kits also lead into our monthly online live Q&A sessions and access to live virtual and in-person lessons about making jam, fermented vegetables, kimchi, and salsa. The goal is to be able to sell these educational packages to people all over the world, since preserving crosses all nationalities and countries. We keep on farming and making the shelf-stable jarred goods that people have loved over these almost twenty years in business.

AS A SEASONED BUSINESS OWNER, TEAMS ARE NECESSARY

As I enter the farm's nineteenth busy farming season, I am analyzing our business growth. I have a great team at the cooperative kitchen helping me create our delicious jarred goods. A collaboration with a spice company (veteran run) helps make my pickle kits. A co-packer helps me create massive volumes of salsa, dill relish, and sriracha pickles, which we can't produce in the kitchen based on our limited womanpower. I now have a website designer who I connect with every year to work on the website and institute marketing strategies for the online courses. All these jobs that I have handed off to others have strengthened the business to a new level. This level has also reduced my stress so I don't feel like I am doing everything.

CONFIDENCE IS EVERYTHING

I am an introvert who became an extrovert in public. I have survived my own hell of depression by doing something I love and spending a lot of time with my family. Confidence is the key to enter the unknown. If it feels scary, that might be a good thing. It probably means you are breaking away from an old life that isn't as satisfying. If you have an idea you can turn into a money-making business, take the reins and make your future yours.

 DON'T FOLLOW THE BEATEN PATH IF THAT'S NOT WHERE YOU WANT TO GO.

There used to be blueprints for life that we were given in high school, but those plans can be redrawn into the future you want. Little did I know when I was five years old that my blueprint was a coloring book depicting a family farm life! You can plant the seeds for your own destiny. I know you can do this. I have!

Chapter
NINE

BOLD MOVES
AND BIG DREAMS

*To my sister and best friend, Michelle, who has stood by my side through every season. To my parents, Michael and Delaila, whose unconditional love and courage built the path for me. To Nick, for your love and support and always reminding me of just how **rich** we truly are. To Olivia and Leo, for the light, laughter, and joy you bring to my life. And with deep gratitude to my beautiful circle of family and friends for lifting me higher and believing in me.*

DR. DANIELLE PAES

Danielle is a passionate pharmacist and changemaker who leads with heart. She's recognized for her unique ability to connect people, ideas, and purpose to drive meaningful change in healthcare. As a consultant, speaker, mentor, and coach, Danielle brings both vision and vulnerability to her work—helping others find courage in uncertainty and possibility in new ways of thinking. Led by faith, intuition, and creativity, she's built a career guiding leaders and organizations to reimagine care through a lens of innovation, equity, and human connection. Grounded, curious, and endlessly optimistic, Danielle believes the boldest moves create the biggest impact—and make the best stories.

@daniellepaes_global

LIFE IS FULL OF OPPORTUNITIES—A STRONG MINDSET WILL HELP YOU SEE THEM AND YOUR PASSION WILL HELP YOU SEIZE THEM!

@daniellepaes_global

The messages I received from women around the world came as a surprise. There was one from Jordan, another from Zimbabwe, and even one from the village in Goa where my grandmother was born. Strangers from different corners of the globe were taking time to express their excitement and celebrate that I had accepted the position of Chief Pharmacist Officer at the Canadian Pharmacists Association. These notes were touching, thoughtful, and humbling. They were a clear reminder of how far women have come, and also, how far we still have to go. It shouldn't be such a big deal—a young woman in a senior executive role—but it is. Because it's still all too uncommon.

I often think of the bright, bold, and potential-filled women who came before me, those who were not given the same schooling or opportunities I was. It was their vision, sacrifices, and courage that paved the path that got me here. I know education is a privilege many women are still not afforded, and that's why I am determined to put mine to good use.

This chapter is a personal reflection on my life shared through a collection of lessons I've learned as I followed my dreams . . .

LIFE IS FULL OF OPPORTUNITIES

Like many who now call Canada home, my mother and father gave up everything they'd ever known to come here. They left their jobs, their family, friends, and the comforts of a familiar life and started over. They did this to offer my sister and me opportunities for a better life. And so, from an early age, I learned to value every opportunity presented to me. I was determined to make sure their sacrifice was not in vain.

The desire to make my family proud has always been with me. I suspect it's ingrained in many of us, especially those whose families immigrated here. As a third-culture kid, my identity has been shaped from a fascinating place of intersecting worlds. Although we are of Goan descent, my family is from Kenya and it's where I was born. We moved to the east end of Toronto when I was very young. I have fond memories of my childhood: Swahili music and warm mandazis, cultural socials and family rosaries, hip-hop and the Scarborough bluffs. My identity is a rich mosaic of Portuguese-infused Indian, African, and Canadian cultures—this is clear to me now. In many ways, it's helped me relate to people from all walks of life . . . it's also made me a bit of a shape-shifter. Looking back, I can see how the ambiguity of my identity allowed me to pass through many filters of unconscious bias. It's a privilege I didn't realize I had. In fact, it wasn't until I reached a level of career success that many were amazed by that I started to pay more attention. *How did I get here? Why am I here and others who look like me aren't?* While women make up more than 60 percent of pharmacists in Canada, those from our BIPOC community are significantly underrepresented in leadership roles. I was a "pattern disruptor," so whether I was ready for it or not, representation became part of my calling, and I embraced the responsibility to be a visible symbol of possibility for thousands.

Lesson: Life is full of opportunities—a strong mindset will help you see them and your passion will help you seize them!

STAY CURIOUS—LIVE AND LEARN

I attended an all-girls Catholic high school. It was a safe and supportive environment to learn, and I thrived both academically and socially. It was here that I developed a strong sense of self and where I gained confidence in my abilities. So, when I ventured off to university to earn my chemistry degree, I was unfazed by the fact that I was one of only three girls in the program. In fact, I wore it as a badge of honor.

Upon graduation, I secured a position with a global pharmaceutical company. By society's standards, I was on track for career success. After a few years of working, I was ready for the next challenge. And as much as I knew the logical next step was to begin my climb up the corporate ladder, that idea didn't excite me. It was safe and expected. I've always been a dreamer and a little unconventional, so I listened to my intuition and did something bold. I took a calculated risk and went back to school to become a pharmacist. It didn't make sense to many, but it did to me. Pharmacy married my passion for science, my love of people, and my desire for impact. So, I put all my savings toward tuition and invested in another four years of education. I can confidently say, it was one of the best decisions I've ever made.

In pharmacy school, I was very intentional about living my education beyond the classroom. No longer chasing grades, I was there for the learning, the experiences, and the connections. I was getting to do university all over again but with the wisdom of real-world work experience. I took advantage of opportunities, but I also put myself out there and created them. I joined clubs, was on student council, entered business-pitch competitions, and even cofounded a health-tech start-up company. I said yes to new experiences, especially those that took me out of my comfort zone. The more I achieved, the more confidence I built, and the bolder my moves got.

As valedictorian of my graduating class, I challenged my colleagues to use their knowledge and privileged position for good. I believed (and still do) that each one had within them the power to change their patients' lives and help heal our communities, and I wasn't afraid to say it! I didn't know it then, but the call to use my voice would be a common thread throughout my professional career and it would form the foundation of my leadership journey.

Lesson: Stay curious—live and learn. You will never know everything, because circumstances, situations, and people all change. The person you are today will develop as you experience the world. Embrace that growth and it will refine you into the best version of yourself.

BELIEF CAN BE BORROWED

Motivated to apply my education in creative and purposeful ways, after graduation I joined a technology company. How's that for unconventional?! My intention was to better understand and influence the design of solutions to support patient care. Before long, I was ready to conquer the next challenge—so fueled by my love for learning, I returned to school to earn my doctor of pharmacy (PharmD) degree. I then landed my dream role practicing as a pharmacist at a pediatric hospital in Toronto, a role that truly shaped me as a clinician. Working on the complex continuing care unit and as part of a high-functioning pharmacy team was extremely rewarding. It was clinically stimulating and collaborative, and my days were filled with professional growth. It was the perfect fit. I felt I had finally found an environment I could settle into. But, of course, the desire for a new challenge soon returned; this time, however, having checked off many professional achievements, I decided to turn my attention to my personal life. I was ready to take on the ultimate test—motherhood!

Being a mother unlocked a level of joy and fulfillment that has been unmatched. During my maternity leave I embraced two births—that of my daughter and that of the new version of me. I cherished the protected time with my baby and the gift of parenthood. The funny thing about life, though, is that you don't get to choose when opportunity comes knocking, and for me, it came at what I thought was the worst possible time. When my daughter was about two months old, I received a call asking if I would be interested in applying for a new high-profile senior executive role. Imagine me, a sleep-deprived, newly minted mother in the middle of a global pandemic. It didn't make sense, and it's not how I would have written it, but it's how it happened. Not only did I not think I was ready for such a role, but I also didn't know if it's what I wanted. As I contemplated the opportunity, I knew it would be an ambitious undertaking and I'd be challenged each day to find a sustainable way to be a wife, mother, sister, daughter, and friend alongside my career. I felt the pressure society places on career-oriented women to be everything to everyone, and it was daunting. I remember weighing all the pros and cons with my husband to determine whether this was the "right" decision for our family. Despite having an extremely supportive partner who encouraged me to go for it, I still wrestled internally with the decision. I felt I had to choose between caring for my child or advancing my career. And as I debated, I felt guilt, wondering which I would regret more.

The decision came down to the fact that I wanted my daughter to know her mother was courageous and made bold moves, even though she was scared. I wanted her to have big dreams for herself and never doubt what she is capable of. And I wanted to show her that you can achieve anything you set your mind to, especially when your faith is stronger than your fears. This was something I learned from my grandmother, who was an incredible woman and taught me so much. I was doing it for the generation of women who came before me who were limited in what they were allowed to achieve, and for the next generation of women who I hope will never know such limits. So, I cut my maternity leave short, and I went for it!

Lesson: Belief can be borrowed—so in those times of uncertainty, turn down the volume on your self-doubt and let the voices of your biggest cheerleaders give you the courage you need to move into action.

FIND YOUR PURPOSE

My role as Chief Pharmacist Officer (CPO) was a dream come true; I loved it! I will be forever grateful for the many lessons it taught me, even the tough ones. Being CPO allowed me to grow in new ways.

It taught me how to use my voice, share my ideas, and advocate for what I believe in. It enabled me to inspire change. I had a platform to represent my profession (over 50,000 pharmacists) at the highest levels of government in Canada. I spoke to media, published articles, and sat on advisory committees. As an influential industry leader, I participated in discussions that had real-world implications on healthcare. It was an incredible privilege, and I knew it. Through my role, I saw an opportunity to redefine what leadership looked like, sounded like, and felt like. I was committed to being authentically me, because it's not enough to be at the table, you need to be comfortable being yourself in that seat. I made it a point to open as many doors for as many people as I could, offering opportunities to individuals who traditionally would have not been invited. I was deliberate in my actions to amplify voices, was generous with my time, and made sure whoever I spoke to felt seen and heard. All their voices mattered, and I knew if they were able to borrow my belief in them to bolster their belief in themselves, they'd soar to new heights. And that's exactly what happened!

I know my purpose is linked to helping others recognize their agency and live to their potential, so I hope my story inspires you to dream big, to take risks, and to lead your life with courage and conviction.

Lesson: Find your purpose. Discover your unique strengths. Be authentic and own what makes you, YOU. Your uniqueness differentiates you, so don't try to fit in, try to stand out!

YOUR INTUITION IS A POWERFUL COMPASS

I recently closed this beautiful chapter in my career, and I did so with a great deal of intention. I left my C-suite executive role, recognized as one of Canada's Top 100 Most Powerful Women, feeling a sense of pride and accomplishment. By most markers of success, I'd achieved it. And yet, I knew there was more. It was time to move on and I was ready, and so even without a clear plan for what came next, I embraced the opportunity for growth in navigating the uncertainty. My faith in myself has always been greater than my fear of the unknown. So, instead of jumping into another high-profile executive role, and there were many to choose from, I trusted my instincts and chose to hit pause. To take a moment for myself. To reflect about who I am, where I came from, and where I want to go. And so here I am, in a moment of quiet reflection, ready to write the next chapter in my story. Feeling that familiar nudge pulling me toward something greater. Remembering the lessons I've learned along the way and ready to reconnect with my dreams.

Lesson: Your intuition is a powerful compass. When things seem off or when you start to feel misaligned, listen. The world is loud, noisy, and full of distractions, but your guide, the ultimate navigation system, lies within you. If it means pressing pause to hear it, then do it!

DON'T STOP DREAMING

It's not lost on me that I'm currently living the life I once dreamed of. In fact, every bold move I've made has come from leaving one dream in pursuit of the next. So, please continue to dream.

 NOTHING IS STATIC; WE ARE CONSTANTLY LEARNING, GROWING, AND EVOLVING AS PEOPLE, AND SO SHOULD OUR DREAMS.

The key is to always be moving closer to becoming who you truly are. For me, that means continuing to live with kindness and compassion and advocating for humanity, because the world needs more of it. In a digital age where our brains are being rewired to not have to think, being human is our superpower. And we are strongest together, so surround yourself with good people and leverage the power of community. Compete less; collaborate more. There's a wise adage that says: *If you want to go fast, go alone, but if you want to go far, go together.*

Life has seasons, and I'm excited about the one I'm stepping into. Although I don't know exactly how it will unfold, I do know I'm dreaming big because the life I've imagined keeps getting better and better. I also know it can be true for you too. You just have to be willing to take risks and always bet on yourself!

For the women reading this, especially the women of color, know there is a place for you at the highest levels of organizations and governments in many countries. The road isn't smooth and the doors are not always wide open but have confidence in yourself and know the value of your perspective in the rooms where decisions are being made.

Chapter
TEN

THE PURSUIT OF
HAPPINESS

In loving memory of my parents, who taught me discipline, drive, appreciation, and resilience through the good and bad times. To my children, Kyle and Angelina, who were the catalyst for my mindset shift and inspired me to make significant changes to become a better parent. Finally, my heartfelt gratitude to my spouse, Jimmy, for having the belief in me to turn my dream into a reality, with constant love and support.

DR. JUDI LUTTIERI

As a formally trained dancer and fitness instructor, Judi developed a profound appreciation for the body and its incredible potential, inspiring her to obtain her doctor in physical therapy. After a long career in pediatrics, orthopedics, and geriatrics, Judi sought further growth and fulfillment by enrolling in a health and life coaching program. The combination of both fields proved to be a game changer in creating lasting change and reinforced her belief that being healthy is a mindset and that prevention is the key to overall well-being. She now owns and operates All in Health & Wellness, a studio where she shares her wealth of experience for mind-body health with her clients.

@Allinhealthmindandbody

ONE OF THE BENEFITS
OF GAINING CLARITY
AROUND WHAT YOU
WANT TO DO IS ALLOWING
YOUR MISSION TO ALIGN
WITH YOUR VALUES
AND STRENGTHS.

@Allinhealthmindandbody

The pursuit of happiness begins when you recognize you are unfulfilled yet drawn to the excitement that life has to offer. Does the universe have its own timing, or is your feeling of despair so strong that the only option is to move forward to possibilities that await a life you never thought you would live?

THE IMPETUS FOR CHANGE

The catalyst always lay dormant in the back of my mind growing up with a mother struggling with mental health issues. Irrational behavior seemed normal to me, and as a child, I didn't realize that isolation and lack of community were unusual. Reflecting on my past, I see how every day was an effort for her to complete her daily routine, and rational thinking was overshadowed by her own childhood trauma. When my mom was only thirteen, her mother died tragically when she was hit by a bus. Sadly, my mom was the only one who could identify her body at the morgue. It must have been incredibly traumatic. I recall her having difficulty accepting affection. The memory is still vivid of me saying the words "I love you" and her responding with silence.

Perhaps her life had shaped her own vulnerabilities into armor. Did she shut down emotionally when she was still a child herself? Or did she not know how to let herself care? I never got to find out. It was a broken relationship that we just started to work on and never got to fully repair. She was known to neglect her health and passed away suddenly.

Her death was the initial moment I realized I did not want my life to mirror hers. I didn't want to be unhappy and unfulfilled. I didn't want to merely survive; I wanted to thrive in life and truly enjoy my friends, family, and experiences. And I didn't want my challenges to derail or define me. What could I do differently that would change this trajectory?

Looking back, I realize she was doing the best she could with the emotional burden she carried, but I wanted to have a closer relationship with my children. I would strive to say the words "I love you" to my own children, and to hear the words from them, and to parent with intention, tenderness, and courage. I would craft a path for my children to speak and be heard, to love and be loved without hesitation.

My mom taught me incredible strength, resilience, and independence, but the inability to show or feel love was the piece that was missing. I knew the stakes were high, the lessons learned of the past should illuminate the way forward, but I was stifled by my own fears and sense of inadequacy. I could only see my lack. A parent's reserved emotional demeanor can be interpreted by the child as them not being good enough. Was that the tape I kept playing in my head?

THE MIND-BODY CONNECTION

We often allow fear to influence our lives, giving it significant power and control, which can result in a hesitation to pursue our goals. I wanted real change but didn't know how to achieve it, so I sought out self-help podcasts, books, and any material I could get my hands on. I began to understand that I couldn't give my own children what they needed because I didn't have what I needed.

The mind has incredible influence, and learning about the mind's vast intricacy, I realized the mind must be trained just like the body. The amygdala, which is our emotional part of the brain, is very primitive, designed to keep us safe. However, not all thoughts should trigger that part of the brain. We can decide what we want to think. After years of training my body in dance and fitness, I never thought that the mind could be trained the same way! The mind-body connection is so powerful, and I began to really ask myself specific questions around my fears, my desires, and my wants. I slowly pushed past those emotionally uncomfortable areas that would block my progress, and I became hopeful about the journey.

When I was young, I was drawn to dance. I didn't realize the profound emotional benefits at the time, other than it made me happy releasing any mental and physical restraints. Now I know that movement is medicine. Your body is designed to move, and when you are immobile, it will rebel. Movement allows you to feel good by releasing endorphins, improving bone health, increasing efficiency in the body, and staying healthy.

Wanting to understand the body better, I pursued a career in physical therapy, and for twenty-seven years, I taught people how to heal their injuries, get stronger, and create a life of movement. Seeing pain and struggle firsthand, I witnessed how movement can transform mental and physical abilities. Having had two children and exercising consistently through both pregnancies, I knew the incredible power of health and discipline. Those experiences solidified my belief that movement is not just a tool for healing but a foundation for growth and resilience. I knew my children's lives would be rooted in movement and encouraged them to explore their own physical potential at a young age.

PAY ATTENTION TO THE SIGNS

As I worked with my own patients, I noticed a lack of sustainable improvement strategies that would carry over post-treatment. A follow-up call to check in would leave me disappointed since the carry-over with good exercise habits and lifestyle changes they previously learned gradually dissipated. I realized that meaningful, sustainable progress often depends on personalized interventions and ongoing support.

Although I had worked in every aspect of care in outpatient and hospital settings, my job at this time was in a home-care agency focusing on quality of treatment and outcomes as the quality care manager. I focused on patient analytics and outcomes to determine how we could give the best care with sustainable results. What would prevent people from going back into the hospital or which outcome trends were most successful. How we could improve by using additional assessment tools, asking specific questions, and improved communication among team members. As we began our training, COVID-19 hit. This pandemic left people very sick in ways we expected but also in ways we did not. We had to utilize whatever strategies we had to help the patient during this strange and scary time.

Trust is a vital component in facilitating transformation, both in the relationship between the patient and healthcare provider and within the patient's self-trust. The level of resistance encountered will determine the type of support required. You must meet patients where they are and work to restore strength, mobility, and hope in those whose bodies were battered by the disease and consequences.

I realized that to drive positive outcomes in patient care, it's crucial to address the mindset of patients and clinicians, to create a bridge in education and implementation, but what was the missing piece with the consistency of maintaining that positive change? I realized I wanted to have a greater impact on lives, empowering and instilling a proactive approach to prevention rather than treatment.

AHA! That was the moment it all came together! I had dreamed of owning my own business my whole career, but it was not a physical therapy office I wanted. It was a comprehensive approach to prevention that would allow patients to gain a deep understanding of their own body, how to listen to messages, then build their ability to create better habits for a healthier lifestyle. This would allow them to have more energy and efficiency daily and feel good!

BELIEVING IN MYSELF

As I embarked on my own certification in coaching, I gained incredible insight into food, lifestyle, and strategies. I began to feel alive, engaged, and hopeful. I started to believe in myself and my dream of owning a business that would be completely aligned with my values and my journey. I realized through my training that nutrition plays such a big role in your energy level, and my relationship with food was not great. Thin was in and I'd been afraid to eat!

The knowledge I was gaining was great information to share with my clients. I began to see the relationship food had in sustaining your blood sugar throughout the day and the crashes from not eating were a way of self-sabotage. Reverting to old habits that were safe whether it was healthy or not. That is the brain's way of saying I would rather do something I know even if the action is not healthy. These were the same emotions I felt through a good part of my own life. Could it be that even though I was trained extensively in nutrition through my education, my mindset overshadowed my common sense? Yes! I realized my knowledge base was repressed by the socialization from my childhood dancing days of not eating. Well, what a change when I began eating full meals and saying yes to carbs at every meal. Not only did I feel great, but I was at a weight I desired.

 YOUR BODY DOES NOT LIE, AND IT WILL TELL YOU EVERYTHING YOU NEED TO KNOW.

Most of the time, we don't listen to our bodies. Perhaps we don't want to know the truth. We will use our coping mechanisms to override that information regardless of whether we feel good about what we are doing. We would rather stay with what is familiar no matter the lack of benefit rather than go into the unknown. That is the brain at its best, keeping us "safe" by staying the same and where we are rather than being uncertain and moving toward somewhere possibly better.

I began journaling and plotting my business. I envisioned it being a wellness studio with exercise and coaching. I was not sure how this was going to happen, but I wanted to create a business to help others and also inspire my children to always look to strive to be the best version of themselves even though it was not going to be easy. I knew the time was right and I was not going to look back. I became laser focused on finally creating my life the way I wanted to and would trust in the process. I knew I would have to get out of my own head and use every lesson whether successful or not as a stepping stone to my next move and not let it deter me. I was going to take action every day no matter how small it was in creating the business. I would learn along the way and not give up until it was done.

TAKING ACTION

I reached out to a successful business coach, Lianne Kim, and set up a strategy call. I knew from our initial encounter that she would be the coach for me. What I lacked in business expertise, I made up for with my experience, my passion, and my determination to surround myself with proven leaders to teach and encourage me. She created a great program that complemented and incorporated the classes I was teaching.

One of the benefits of gaining clarity around what you want to do is allowing your mission to align with your values and strengths. You need to do the work both mentally and physically to stay on track and keep evolving. You will gain incredible momentum from your clarity, consistency, and calmness: the three drivers to allow you to move forward.

1. **Clarity:** I would say the most important thing to do is to be clear about what your mission is and what you want to do. Spend time asking yourself questions, diving deep into any barriers, seeking external help when you need support.

2. **Consistency:** Show up every day for yourself and do the work, no matter what your emotions are telling you. Stick to the plan and work on your business daily.

3. **Calmness:** Stress is a deterrent. Learn to do deep breathing, meditate, walk, and stay outdoors. Shut out anything that takes you away from that calm mindset. Exercise daily and you can change that energy.

It has been less than a year and I am currently the CEO of All in Health and Wellness, a fitness studio that utilizes physical therapy best practice exercises and the Pilates reformers for the ultimate body experience. It allows individuals to create a strong core, efficient muscle, and gain strength, flexibility and balance. It is complemented by a coaching program that ensures proper eating, strategies for stress and action, and an overall transformative process. I have grown into a business with a strong community, and my mission is to create a fusion with the mind and body approach to allow individuals to stay healthy, happy, and forever evolving.

Looking back, it feels as though every step, every challenge, and every breakthrough was leading me to this moment. From my struggles with nutrition and self-belief to the determination that fueled my journey, I can see now how every twist and turn shaped the vision I had for All in Health and Wellness. It's not just a business, it's the embodiment of resilience, growth, and the deep understanding that transformation is a lifelong practice.

The happiness I see on my clients' faces when they realize their own strength, the gratitude they express when they find balance, and the confidence they gain through our work together—these are the moments that make it all worthwhile. Each story, each success, reflects the path I walked and the lessons I learned. What began as a personal struggle has become a shared journey, a community built on the foundation of health, mindfulness, and empowerment.

As I sit in my studio today, reflecting on how far I've come, I feel an unparalleled sense of fulfillment. I've created a space where people can reconnect with their bodies, rediscover their potential, and rewrite their own narratives. And in doing so, I've rewritten mine. The dream I had of combining physical wellness and coaching has come to life, and it continues to grow, evolve, and inspire.

This isn't the end of the story, it's a new beginning. I've come full circle, from uncertainty to clarity, from struggle to strength, from vision to reality. My relationship with my own children has flourished with love, respect, and admiration, which is another dream come true. It is a work in progress, and through it all, I've learned that resilience is not just about rising after a fall but about stepping forward each day with purpose, gratitude, and joy. Here's to the next chapter, and to the endless possibilities that come with a heart open to growth and happiness.

Chapter ELEVEN

I WASN'T LIKE EVERYONE ELSE—AND THAT WASN'T ALWAYS A BAD THING

To Arya, my spark, my joy, and the reason behind it all; to Alex, my partner in crime—in parenting, business, and life; and to my parents and brother, for loving me unconditionally from the very beginning.

ERIN TEE

Erin is a neurodiversity advocate, educator, and visual media specialist who designs inclusive visual content and learning experiences through a neurodiversity-affirming lens. With an MEd in Cognitive Diversity and lived experience as a neurodivergent parent of a twice-exceptional child, Erin blends storytelling with education to spark understanding and change. Backed by twenty-five years in media production, she creates resources, courses, and presentations for families, educators, and organizations. In addition to her creative and educational work, Erin offers one-on-one consultations and small group sessions, providing practical strategies and compassionate support for parents, educators, and professionals working with neurodivergent children.

@erinktee

YOU DESERVE
A PLACE IN THE WORLD
THAT FITS YOU,
NOT ONE THAT
CONSTANTLY ASKS
YOU TO CHANGE.

@erinktee

The summer I turned twelve, I got my period, visited friends in France, and discovered Madonna's *Like a Prayer CD*. It was also the summer I started feeling deeply misunderstood, like I was different from everyone around me. Sure, some of that was puberty. But a bigger part was that I didn't think or feel like everyone else. I was the first one in my small grade 7 class to get breasts, and honestly, it felt awful. Suddenly all the boys I'd been joking with and challenging to arm wrestle in the library the year before were now looking at me differently. I started listening to music obsessively. I dreamed of growing up to be Madonna because she made standing out feel powerful. She had that energy, that grit. It was as if she said: *Being different means you're destined for more.* That message stayed with me.

By grade 8, I found my sanctuary: a weekend theater school called Kids-in-Action. I spent my teen years living and breathing musical theater. It saved me. It gave me a space to be loud, weird, and hyper-fixated on things like *Les Misérables* and Madonna without being the odd one out. That theater school reminded me that high school wasn't everything; I had my world outside of it and belonged there. I was lucky to find "my people," the ones who shared my passions or intensity. I wasn't alone, even if I didn't quite fit.

I didn't have a name for it then, but I was already figuring out how to design a life around what brought me joy. Musical theater wasn't just an interest—it was a regulation strategy, a social workaround, and a self-confidence builder. In short, it was a lifeline.

Looking back, I see all the signs. I had intense sensory sensitivities, especially around food and sound. I hated unexpected transitions. I had deep, obsessive interests. I was loud. Bossy. Talkative. I didn't like being told what to do or who to be. But I didn't see these things as a problem. They were part of what made me *me*. I could also "do" school well. I got good grades, was quick to memorize, and had teachers who often saw the best in me. I also grew up in a family that loved me unconditionally. So, I never questioned my brain. I just figured I was creative and driven

But then I became a parent.

MY CHILD: THE SPARK

When my child was five, they began having a really hard time meeting classroom expectations. They were fidgety, transitions were a nightmare, and they appeared not to be paying attention. Their teacher and early childhood educator couldn't make sense of it—they were articulate, advanced in reading, and clearly intelligent, but they couldn't sit on the carpet or follow directions. By February, we were facing school refusal, chronic meltdowns, and even tics. It broke my heart.

We started the long journey into assessments—ADHD, anxiety, Tourette's—and eventually ended up in a psychiatrist's office. The evaluation revealed significant sensory processing differences, something that often goes unseen but shapes how they experience the world.

What helped most wasn't a diagnosis but a shift in how we understood and supported them. It was a quieter classroom with movement breaks and a teacher who saw my child's spark instead of their disruption. At our first parent-teacher meeting that year, he said: "So they can't sit still on the carpet . . . that's something *I* need to get over."

That moment stayed with me. The problem wasn't my child. The problem was the box they were being asked to fit into.

As I researched how to support them, a spark was ignited. I became obsessed with understanding neurodivergent brains. I read everything I could find, watched lectures, and fell down rabbit holes about executive functioning, sensory regulation, and twice-exceptionality. I realized I wasn't just trying to understand my child, I was uncovering a deep and growing passion for understanding neurodiversity.

The more I learned, the more I realized: working *with* a neurodivergent brain means throwing out much of what we're taught about success and discipline. It's not about forcing change through willpower. It's about noticing patterns (what supports regulation, what sparks interest, what leads to connection) and then designing around that.

ENTER BRIDGES: A LEAP TOWARD MYSELF

Fast-forward to 2021, and I stumbled upon the Bridges Graduate School of Cognitive Diversity in Education. As I scrolled through the website, a voice in my head whispered, *This is it.* I'd already been deep-diving into brain research, educational psychology, and strength-based learning frameworks. I thought—if I'm already doing all this learning, why not do it *formally*? Why not earn the letters that let me create resources in my own voice, without needing someone else to be the "expert"?

So, I applied. I was terrified.

I wasn't a teacher, and I had no formal education in "education." I was a video producer, but I took the leap, and it was one of the best decisions of my life.

From the first course, I stretched my brain in ways I hadn't in a long time. I met some of the most brilliant, warm, and committed people I'd ever encountered—educators, therapists, and specialists who were all there for the same reason: to better support the kids who are too often misunderstood or missed, oftentimes because they were parents to those kids. And sometimes because they were those kids. As I learned more about diverse learning profiles, twice-exceptionality, and strength-based pedagogy, I also started to see myself more clearly.

Bridges was never just about my child. It was also about me starting to discover the authentic me.

LEADING WITH CURIOSITY (AND A LOT OF TRIAL AND ERROR)

I do this work today as a creator, advocate, and educator because I believe deeply in a world where neurodivergent people feel whole.

Bridges helped me find language and community. It gave me the foundation to understand not just my child, but systems. And it helped me reclaim something I didn't even know I needed: the right to show up exactly as I am. From there, it's been a slow but steady shift toward building a life rooted in acceptance, curiosity, and self-compassion.

Every day, I try to lean into understanding not just for others but also for myself. And when internalized ableism creeps in, when that voice whispers that I *should* be able to do things differently or more easily, I pause. I challenge it. I ask: "Whose rules am I following right now? Who am I trying to impress?"

Parenting has taught me more than any course ever could. So much of the "by-the-book" advice didn't work for us. Trusting my instinct has made all the difference. I can now anticipate when my child might be getting overwhelmed. I see the signs. And more importantly, they're learning to see them too. They're learning how to ask for downtime. They're learning that their needs are not inconveniences.

A LIFE THAT FITS

We've created a rhythm in our home that works for *us*: low-demand weekends, time alone when we need it, time together when it feels right. We worry less about what people might think if they could see us. We're not parenting for optics—we're parenting for connection, authenticity, and a life that feels aligned. I have a relationship with my child that feels real and whole, and I am beyond grateful.

Through learning how to support them, I've learned how to better care for myself. How can I show up for them, especially as a safe, steady co-regulator, if I'm already out of spoons? I've realized that self-care is essential, but not how I used to think. I don't mean yoga, spa days, or working out (unless that's your thing). I mean: What brings you joy? What helps you come back to yourself?

One of my biggest shifts is learning to tune into my capacity or check in on my spoons. Spoon theory is a way of thinking about energy as a limited resource. Each task, physical, emotional, and social, costs a spoon. And when you're out, you're out. Neurodivergent capacity can fluctuate significantly based on sleep, sensory load, transitions, emotions, etc. I've started checking in with myself regularly: How's my energy? Where's my focus? What does my nervous system need—movement, stillness, silence, connection? Regulation isn't something I do *after* I fall apart. It's something I build into my day. When I listen to my capacity and plan accordingly, I get more done and feel less overwhelmed.

I've discovered that the number one regulation technique for me, especially when I'm feeling overwhelmed, is singing musical theater songs. And not just any songs—specific ones, in a particular key, with notes that hit just right. It took me a while to realize that my deep love of singing, first unlocked when I was twelve, wasn't just a passion, it was a form of nervous system regulation. It's what helps me feel whole, grounded, and joyful.

LEARNING TO LISTEN TO MY BRAIN AND BODY

Working with my brain means paying attention to when I feel most focused, most creative, most calm. I've learned to notice what lights me up, what drains me, and where my natural rhythms fall. I don't try to force deep work when I'm mentally fried, and I don't schedule back-to-back meetings if I know I need recovery time in between. I batch creative work for when I'm most energized and build white space into my day to breathe.

I KEEP A RUNNING LIST OF TASKS THAT MATCH DIFFERENT ENERGY STATES—THINGS I CAN DO WHEN I'M SHARP AND FOCUSED, AND THINGS I CAN DO WHEN I'M FOGGY OR OVERSTIMULATED.

I've also gotten better at building in buffer time, because transitions take energy, and I don't always bounce between tasks the way others do. This isn't about productivity hacks, it's about designing a life I can sustain. A life that works for me, not against me.

This is my life now. It may not be perfect, but it is real, full, and meaningful. I listen to what my brain and body tell me, and I choose joy and regulation over shame and "should haves." For a long time, I chased productivity in ways that didn't suit me—I used to say to myself "just get through this and then you can rest . . ." but the rest never came. I was always pushing through tasks, trying to stay consistent just because I thought I was supposed to. I don't need to wake up at 5 a.m. to be successful. I don't need to have the same routine every day to be consistent. I let go of most "shoulds" unless they serve me.

One helpful question I often ask myself is: *Who is this expectation serving?* If the answer isn't "me" or "my family," I pause. Just because something is common or typical doesn't mean it's right for me. I don't need to mimic neurotypical routines to live a good life. My goal isn't to fit in. Letting go of external expectations has been key to building a sustainable, joyful rhythm that lets me thrive *on my terms*.

SELF-ADVOCACY, WITHOUT APOLOGY

I'm also learning to ask for what I need—without feeling I need to apologize. Whether it's requesting quiet space at an event, taking a sensory break at a party, or saying no to last-minute plans, I advocate for what keeps me regulated. I've also gotten clearer with clients and collaborators about how I work best. Boundaries aren't about shutting people out. They're about protecting the energy I need to show up fully.

And that's something I want to model for my kid too.

You don't have to be someone else to be worthy of care. The way your brain works is valid. You are not broken. You deserve dignity, respect, and belonging, whatever that looks like for you.

And you are allowed to build a life that works *for you*. That's the message I want to keep creating, sharing, and amplifying.

Today, I create resources, courses, and media that help others see neurodiversity not through a deficit lens but as a regular, beautiful part of human diversity. Neurodivergent brains are *whole*, with all the strengths and struggles that come with them. That's just it: We wouldn't be who we are without both sides of the coin.

UNMASKING, RECLAIMING, BELONGING

For years, I tried to be more polished, predictable, and palatable. I didn't realize how often I was masking until I stopped. I connect with people better when I'm not pretending to be someone else. One of my greatest strengths in my business is my ability to connect authentically with people, to understand what my client needs, or to help an interview subject feel safe on camera. I lead with curiosity and honesty. I don't share everything with everyone, but I no longer hide who I am.

I'm not interested in fitting in. I'm interested in belonging and helping to build spaces where others feel safe to show up as they are. And that starts with me doing the same.

It's also an ongoing practice—I still reflect on what's working, what's not, and what I need to adjust. That's part of working with my brain too. Some weeks I need more structure. Some weeks I need more rest. Some days I need a total reset. I don't beat myself up for needing to pivot. Instead, I check in, make the changes I need, and keep moving forward. I don't need a perfect system. I just need one that lets me keep learning, growing, and coming back to myself again and again.

I've stopped chasing the approval of people who don't understand me. If someone can't handle the full version of me, my sensitivity, enthusiasm, and candor, they're probably not my people. And that's okay. I'm happier now than I've ever been. Not because everything's easy but because I've fully embraced my authentic self.

It feels strange to leave you with advice because I don't believe in one-size-fits-all anything. But I will say this, whether you're reading this for yourself, for your child, or for someone you love who's been made to feel broken: You deserve a place in the world that fits you, not one that constantly asks you to change.

You don't have to earn belonging. Your people are out there. Sometimes they're hard to spot—especially when you're exhausted from trying to be someone else. But often, they show up when you start showing up as yourself. Follow what feels real. That's often the way home.

Chapter TWELVE

FINDING A BETTER WAY

To my parents, for always supporting me; to my sister, for being my person and go-to for everything; to my mother-in-law, for being a successful mamaprenuer who always cheers me on; to my husband, whose constant belief in me gives me the confidence to keep going; and to my son: you are my daily inspiration to be better.

JACQUELINE SMITH

Jacqueline is a seasoned travel insurance broker with over two decades of experience specializing in the seniors and snowbird market. After a successful career in the industry, she took the bold step to launch her own brokerage, TripInsure Inc. With her wealth of knowledge and personalized service, Jacqueline is passionate about helping Canadians travel with confidence.

@tripinsureinc

KEEP MOVING FORWARD. FIND YOUR INNER STRENGTH AND BELIEVE IN YOURSELF.

@tripinsureinc

Deciding to become a mother is the best decision I've ever made. The instant and fierce love I felt for the tiny human I just met ignited something inside me that I never knew existed. In the back of my mind, before motherhood, I always knew I could achieve more than what I was already doing with my career, but I was complacent and happy doing the minimums to pay my bills. I've always had a great work ethic, but I thought of working as something you just had to do to pay for your life. Whenever friends or family suggested I start my own company, I'd give a dismissive chuckle and not give it another thought. Then, with my baby son in my arms, came the great responsibility to be better. To strive for more. To be the best mother and role model my child deserved.

The first ten months of maternity leave were quite difficult, to say the least. I was overwhelmed with my new life caring for a newborn, struggling with breastfeeding, battling postpartum depression, healing from minor health issues from pregnancy and childbirth, and trying to study and pass exams that were required to upgrade my license for my job. And on top of all that, my husband and I were house hunting! It was a lot to deal with, especially when you're sleep deprived. It was the most challenging year of my life. But I passed all my exams, regained my health (both physically and mentally), and we bought a house. When we moved in and got settled, I finally began feeling like my old self again. I only really began to enjoy my maternity leave during the last two months, just as it was coming to an end. I wanted to return to work and regain financial independence, but being home with my son gave me a sense of purpose I didn't expect. It finally felt like I was doing something that mattered, and I didn't want to give that up.

June 3, 2019, was my first day back at work and two days before my son's first birthday. As I battled the rush-hour commute to try and pick him up before his daycare closed at 6 p.m., I wondered why my beautiful one-year-old was now going to be "raised" by other women. *Why am I back at work and missing so much of his life? Oh right, I need to make money! Isn't that why most kids are in daycare?* When we got home, I raced to feed him before his bedtime routine and sleep at 7:30. Not only did I just get to see him for an hour and a half in the evening, I got (as most parents know) the crankiest hour and a half of the day! I was well aware that most people I knew lived like this, but I couldn't help but wonder if there was a better way.

FINDING THE SILVER LINING

Fast-forward to March 2020 and the world shut down. While COVID-19 was a stressful and scary time for most (it was for me at first too), it actually gave me the most special gift of quality time. I got to be a part-time stay-at-home mom! With daycare closed and my career as a travel insurance broker coming to a halt, I was only going into the office for half days. I was thankful to still be employed when so many were being let go. The pandemic gave me the time and space to connect with myself and my family in a way I never had before. It slowed down life so I could notice what truly mattered. It reminded me that joy comes from the small, ordinary moments we live every day. Even though we couldn't go anywhere because everything was closed, even though we couldn't see anyone outside our "bubble," I felt grateful for morning cuddles, afternoon walks, doing yoga in my living room during nap time, baking, and making dinner instead of feeling rushed to just throw food on the table. I loved not having endless to-do lists (outside the home) and places to be for that period of time. We could just be us, and I felt so fulfilled by being home taking care of my son. Living through the pandemic also put things in perspective. There were so many people around the world struggling with health problems, losing loved ones, or worrying about how they were going to feed their families. After the initial panic subsided, I felt content and more grateful for what I had. I felt *rich,* not because of money but because we had everything that truly mattered. We had a roof over our heads, food on the table, our health, and love in our home. It was during that time that I got a glimpse of what life could look like with more family time and realized how much better it felt.

THE CATALYST FOR CHANGE

As we came out of the lockdowns and business started to get back to normal, I returned to work. But now the hours were long, and the work environment seemed incredibly stressful. For the first time in nearly twenty years of working in the business and ten at this company, I wasn't enjoying it. I felt like I was stretched thin by being pulled in so many directions. By early fall of 2023, I was so stressed out over work that I dreaded going into the office and began to burn out. I was bringing work home with me and felt consumed by my responsibilities. I was anxious and irritable and started snapping at my family for no reason. I was withdrawn, I did not want to be social, my mind was wandering at night, and I couldn't sleep. I was getting panic attacks, was on the verge of tears all the time, and was depressed.

I knew I needed to get better not only for myself but for my family. I made an appointment with my doctor to discuss my mental health. It was clear to my doctor that my place of employment was the cause of my stress. I was put on sick leave for three weeks, was prescribed medication to help with the anxiety and panic attacks, and was told I should seek therapy. During those three weeks, my symptoms significantly reduced, and I felt lighter. My doctor extended my sick leave for another three weeks, giving me the time I needed to focus on what my next steps would be.

THE INNER SPARK OF STRENGTH

This time around, something hit differently when my family said I should start my own business instead of going back to a place that was making me so unhappy and sick. I did not resign voluntarily; it was a necessary step due to the conditions in which I was faced. Following legal advice, I have omitted details about my former workplace to focus on my personal journey, but suffice to say, I am proud of the strength I showed to stand up for myself and demand accountability. I needed to prioritize my health and happiness.

I also realized that I've never hated what I do, I just started to hate the environment I was doing it in. I am actually really good at my job. I enjoy talking to my clients and hearing about their exciting travel plans and making sure they have the coverage they need to travel with peace of mind. I enjoy helping people. The biggest rewards are when clients tell me that they feel like an actual person and not a number when they call me, and when they proceed to refer me to their friends and family. Having people put trust in you is a powerful feeling. So, if I love my job, then why not do it for myself?

I had a long list of reasons why I couldn't do it:

- I am not a leader.
- I didn't go to a fancy university or get a business degree.
- I can't leave the security of a steady job to start over.
- I don't have the money to open a business and not make any income for the first few years.
- I can't be responsible for everything.
- I'm not strong enough or smart enough to do something like that.
- What if I fail?

But I had even bigger reasons why I had to try:

- I want to spend more quality time with my family.
- I want to be happier.

- I want to be at every school concert, every soccer practice, every hockey game.
- I want to be home with my son when he is sick.
- I want to build my own dreams, not someone else's.
- I want to have a more flexible schedule.
- What if I succeed?

And thankfully, I was also surrounded by an incredible support system who already believed in me. Starting a business has not been the easiest time, but I am confident in my "why." I am proud of the strength I found to start over. As the brilliant comedian and author Hannah Gadsby says, "There is nothing stronger than a broken woman who has rebuilt herself."

This hasn't been an easy journey. I have lots of days of doubt and wonder about whether I have made the right decision to leave the security behind. We were a two-income family, so giving up a guaranteed salary was not an easy decision, but we both agreed that while money is important, it isn't everything.

 WHAT GOOD IS MONEY IF YOU DON'T HAVE QUALITY TIME TO SPEND WITH YOUR LOVED ONES AND YOUR HEALTH IS SUFFERING?

Scaling back on spending until my business provides a stable income is hard sometimes, but just like during the pandemic, knowing that we have everything we need provides comfort and the confidence to continue. This journey has brought me to entrepreneurship and more time for what matters the most—my family.

I knew being a business owner would have its challenges but never fathomed just how hard and lonely some days can be. On those dark days when my confidence is low and my anxieties are high, I have a list of activities I know will help reignite my spark and lift me up.

Maybe these will help you too, if you're ever struggling:

Daily affirmations. I tell myself: "I am confident," "I CAN do this," "I can learn," "I am a strong, resilient woman." Repeating these often really does help.

Exercise. Weight training and yoga are my go-tos. I always feel better afterward and have a clearer mindset. Find something that works for you.

Get outside. Be in nature. Get fresh air. I am lucky enough to have great trails behind my house where I can unwind and breathe deeply. Step away from your computer and stroll through a local park or forest.

Find your support system. I have incredible support from my husband and family. And finding the community of Mamas & Co. has been so helpful. Having other female business owners to connect with who understand the hustle has been truly uplifting. Search out like-minded positive people.

Journal. Get those thoughts and ideas down on paper. Writing brings clarity.

Martini? Sometimes a great cocktail is all you need to unwind! (After work, of course.)

Do you ever feel like there's something more out there for you? Do you want more meaning in your life than just the daily grind you're used to? Don't ignore that feeling in your gut for too long like I did. I wanted to make a move, but I always dismissed the idea because staying in my comfort zone was safer. I didn't want to upset anyone. Don't ever put your life on hold for someone else. Keep moving forward. Find your inner strength and believe in yourself.

Nelson Mandela said, "I never lose. I either win or I learn." I have this phrase written on the whiteboard in my office and read it often. It's how I feel about all the decisions I have made in the last year and will continue to make. Having your own business requires making so many decisions. Some turn out great; others, not so much. But that's how you learn and grow. Becoming a mother gave me the drive to put into action what I only dreamed was possible. For the first time in my life, I feel empowered. I'm not "stuck" anymore. I feel fulfilled knowing that I am building something of my own, and for my family. This is my time, and I will continue to move forward, take chances, and do things that scare me. There will always be difficult days ahead, but I am happy with what I have accomplished so far and the moves I have made. And I'm excited for what I'll do next. I found *my* better way to live. If I can start over, you can too.

Chapter
THIRTEEN

FINDING THE BLESSING
IN THE BURNOUT

To every woman who has ever felt the weight of burnout, may you find the courage to pause, breathe, and reclaim the vibrant life within you. This chapter is for you, and for my daughter, my greatest teacher in resilience and love.

CRYSTAL SAMUELS

Crystal is the founder of Dare to Flow with Me Meditation and Wellness, where she helps others use meditation as a foundational tool to transform their lives. In alignment with the wellness arm of her business, she is also a burnout coach dedicated to supporting women in reclaiming their lives with clarity and intention. Through grounding practices and compassionate guidance, she leads women through her signature five-step framework to break free from burnout, rebuild from within, and elevate their overall well-being—one mindful breath at a time.

@daretoflowwithme

I HAD TO RETRAIN MY MIND TO BELIEVE WHAT IS FACTUAL AND TO LET GO OF THE UNTRUE STORIES I'VE HELD ON TO AND BELIEVED FOR YEARS, DECADES EVEN.

@daretoflowwithme

"Crystal . . . Crystal, are you hearing me? You are in no position to go back to work at this time. I'm writing you a medical note, and I need you to bring it into your workplace to take the next six weeks off."

It was a hot and humid day in July. Not only was it hazy outside, it was also hazy in my mind.

"You are clearly in a state where your body and your mind are exhausted, and you need to rest. Please take this time to recalibrate, and don't worry about anything except making yourself whole again."

My doctor saw me exactly where I was and didn't question me once. She was a gem. But I was questioning myself. So many thoughts were running through my mind, but I couldn't make much sense of them, other than having strong feelings of shame.

"Are you going to submit the doctor's note to your employer?" The worry in her voice was glaring and apparent.

"I . . . I'm not sure."

That was the harsh reality. I wasn't sure of so many things, but the biggest one I wasn't sure of was myself. I felt like such a failure. How had I gotten to this position? I was supposed to have my entire life together. On paper, everything looked perfect, but inside, everything was crumbling.

THE BUILDUP

At the start of 2020, I had my daughter. There were complications during the pregnancy: my tummy started to get smaller instead of getting bigger.

The doctors asked me so many times if I felt water leaking, but I felt nothing of the sort. The only thing I experienced was extreme tiredness in my first trimester. If my belly wasn't visibly getting smaller, I would have thought they were lying about me having complications. I felt my pregnancy was perfect. And what was even more bizarre was there was no formal diagnosis. They thought there might be a small leak in my amniotic fluid, something they equated to a slow leak in a tire. I was really scared. My sweet baby was barely moving except for the faint kicks I felt in the wee hours of the morning when everything was still, peaceful, and quiet. As a result, I was sequestered to bed rest in the hospital for one month prior to birth, but I made the best out of it. I had a wonderful support system around me, I made lots of friends in the hospital, and I relied on prayer for a safe delivery. Thanks to God, my birth process was smooth, and my sweet baby Zyler arrived on January 16.

When the pandemic hit in March, I had some worries about what the world would be like for Zyler and prayed that I didn't bring her into a world that felt like it was about to implode. But overall, the time was a blessing for me and my daughter. While I absolutely acknowledge the difficulty, pain, and loss so many experienced, for me, it was a time to stay home and bond with my baby. There were no external influences or interruptions; it was just me and her rocking it through the pandemic.

I had the privilege of staying home with my daughter for almost two years; twenty months to be exact. During that time off, I thought I'd use part of the time to level up in my career and go for a promotion. I wanted to move up in the organization, so in true Crystal fashion, I pulled out my spreadsheet and started to plan. While I was full-time momming, I was also a master networker having virtual coffee chats during Zyler's nap times, connecting with old and new colleagues, brushing up my résumé, even having practice interviews, then real interviews.

And I did it while holding my baby in one hand, spreadsheet in the other. Two weeks after returning to the workplace, I got the call that I was promoted to a director. Everything was perfect, until it wasn't.

ENTERING THE STORM

When I went back to work, I was working at the same pace as I had been prior to having a child. That meant full workdays, working evenings, and waking up early to put on any finishing touches. You see, I'm a bit of a perfectionist when it comes to my work. I have come to learn that my perfectionism was a trauma response to my perceptions of rejection. I believed that everything just had to be perfect in order to prove to others that I was worthy and valuable.

But no one told me when you have a child in daycare, they get sick every two weeks, which means you're sick every two weeks. And ultimately, there is always at least one person sick in your house all the time!

I was experiencing mind and body exhaustion and entering a perfect storm of burnout. Extreme exhaustion was the first ingredient to this perfect storm.

Next, I was promoted into a new area where I didn't have established relationships, and the one person I thought I could lean on was about to be let go from the organization. For my entire career I was in the tech world, knowing the ins and outs of the business and the players involved. But in this new role, I now needed to know the world of marketing and communication, which was very different for me. It was also very cliquey, and I didn't quite fit in. I tried, but I felt rejected by the community. I spiraled downward fast when the sense of belonging I used to feel was shaky. I had always equated my career with my identity, using my work title to introduce myself. I wanted everyone to see the hardworking, focused Crystal who knew her stuff.

There were a few people who were intimidated by my success and made undermining comments or took subtle actions that led me to question myself at every turn. I began to believe that if my workplace saw me as a failure, then I must be one. I was experiencing an identity crisis, taking validation from a bunch of strangers and losing control of the narrative of how I wanted the world to see me.

This led to the second ingredient in my perfect storm of burnout: the loss of my voice.

There were many instances during my time back in the workplace when I was often at a loss for words and would draw complete blanks. I didn't know why this was happening. I felt like I really wasn't good enough and couldn't answer simple questions. I now know I was experiencing high levels of anxiety. I used to be vibrant and vocal, confidently sharing thoughts and ideas, but that eroded over the months to the point where I would be speechless with nothing to add, afraid of saying the wrong things and being viewed as incompetent.

The third ingredient for the perfect storm was a lack of authentic connection with my true self, a heart-centered compassionate human who loved to ground herself. I was experiencing a disconnect between my thoughts and the identity and brand I had created for myself at work. I wasn't sure how to show up in my environment, and this wasn't just in work meetings but in social settings too. With friends and family, I began to feel awkward, like a fraud, like I didn't belong. The internal turmoil became so real and exhausting that I would feel numb with anxiety and social media scroll myself to sleep.

My boundaries were eroding with others and with myself. It's often said that boundaries are not to keep people away but to help people understand the expectations and healthy parameters needed for building a beautiful relationship that is respectful and trusting. The other side of boundaries often overlooked is that they are the healthy standards we have to create with ourselves.

Subconsciously, I was allowing stories of doubt to cloud my mind. It was like riding in an elevator every day filled with smoke and unbearable music. I was not setting my boundaries and became 100 percent susceptible to my environment, externally and internally. That smoky, unbearable ride became my daily standard. My energy levels plummeted along with beliefs about myself.

The final ingredient to my perfect storm: lack of external and internal boundaries.

Of course, I burned out. I was a first-time mom and solo parent who was promoted to a higher level in my organization with little support. I was exhausted. I didn't even know my true self anymore, and I couldn't find my voice to communicate and share succinct sentences, thoughts, or feelings. My self-doubt was strong, and I felt so misaligned from the true essences of me. I suffered complete burnout.

THE TURNING POINT

If I truly understood my worth, if I truly understood I am not defined by a title, if I truly understood that anything I imagine can come to life, and if I truly understood that the only validation I need is from within, all that occurred to bring me to that moment in my doctor's office wouldn't have ever happened. And this is where the hard work began; this is where I had to be honest with myself. To pull myself out of burnout, I had to do some deep reflection and connect with my true soul's purpose. The crossroads I was at was to either go back to the same psychologically unsafe work environment and avoid my legacy wounds that contributed to getting into that state or to try something different. I was so desperate to move back into a healthy state of mental wellness, and the main driver was my sweet baby Zyler. I had to do it for her, so I voted for something different. And while the motivation should have come from within myself, honestly, it didn't. My desperation to become stronger mentally and then physically came out of my unwavering love for my child, to make sure she would be okay and would have a mommy with a sound mind, body, and spirit..

RECLAIMING AND REBUILDING

With my decision to do things differently, I started with one of the hardest things for people, especially moms, to do: take intentional rest.

Rest, I thought. *How hard can that be?* Very hard, especially when you are used to proving yourself through doing, which is so difficult to unlearn. Then, I decided to grieve my old identity and let it go. I thanked it for what it did for me up to this point, because it protected me for years and gave me the opportunity to build independence and financial stability.

 AS I GRIEVED MY OLD IDENTITY, I GAVE MYSELF THE PERMISSION TO REIMAGINE WHAT LIFE COULD LOOK LIKE FOR ME.

And it did not include anchoring to a role, title, or a different job, but anchoring instead to my authentic self, the real Crystal. The one who lived within me. But I had to search for her again, asking myself questions like: *What lights you up, Crystal? What brings you joy? Where do you need to ask for support so you can have more light and joy in your life?*

And I answered the questions with truth and without limitations on what God could do in my life. Then I had to get to work and set my necessary boundaries. That meant having those tough conversations, and not just with others but with myself too. It was an ongoing and daily process. I had to retrain my mind to believe what is factual and to let go of the untrue stories I've held on to and believed for years, decades even. Along the way, I had to make some space for a glow-up, and by that I mean not only stepping into a new physical look, which included a sexy new haircut, but also my glow that illuminates from within and lights up all rooms I walk into unapologetically. Along this journey, I took action that aligned with my soul's purpose, which is to empower myself and other women to heal through rest, stillness, and intentional self-prioritization, and to reconnect with your authentic and true self.

I was able to get through this storm in my life and reach calmer waters through meditation and prayer. I was able to move through some of my most difficult days, hours, and moments with inward reflection and deep listening. I was able to re-center and come back to myself. I found clarity again in my thoughts and was able to make sound decisions that allowed my purpose to emerge.

I am so proud to be able to now help others with burnout by breaking a cycle that was clearly not working for me anymore. I do this through my one-on-one and group coaching where I help mainly high-achieving women reclaim and rebuild their lives after burnout. After my painful journey through burnout, I recounted step-by-step what I did to find meaningful purpose again in life. I also tested my framework with other women who went through similar experiences, and the test results always led back to these five steps required to move from overwhelm to empowerment:

- Rest your mind and body
- Grieve your old identity
- Reimagine life on your terms
- Rebuild your self-trust
- Elevate and sustain your authentic and true YOU

With all this shared, I want to be transparent that going through these steps was hard as hell. I don't want you to underestimate the vulnerable, raw, and tears-filled emotions I felt. There was a physical manifestation of exhaustion, drain, and brain fog, and it was a messy, uncertain, and revealing process. But at the same time, going through this was expansive, transformative, healing, and empowering.

There was so much blessing in my burnout because through it, my purpose emerged and I became aligned with *me*! I can now show up for myself and my family in ways I would have never imagined before. I am happy with the small, simple moments. And I am a better mom and able to finally prioritize myself, and I can see this for you too. Here's to finding the blessing in the burnout!

Chapter
FOURTEEN

FINDING YOUR PURPOSE
IS A PROCESS

To all bosses who came before Smithery, thanks for preparing me to bet on myself. To my family: Maurice, Amelia, Brooke, Pam, Jim, Kevin, and Hillary—thank you for your belief in my ambition. To our clients, for choosing to shop with a small, woman-powered business. Finally, heaps of gratitude to Mavis for selling me her "baby," to the Smithery Style team for welcoming me so warmly, and to the community of mompreneurs I've met this year for walking with me on my journey. It takes a village to support a small-business owner's dreams, and I am truly blessed to have mine.

SHANNON GALLAGHER

Shannon is the owner of Smithery Style, an e-retailer and style service that helps women "shop their shape." As a small business owner, she uses her career experience in PR, higher education, and marketing to help empower busy women to dress with confidence and comfort. Shannon's "why" is her two daughters, who she hopes will grow up in a world where fashion is inclusive and getting dressed in the morning is a joy.

@smitherystyle

WE ARE OFTEN TOLD IT'S PEOPLE AND NOT THINGS THAT MAKE US TRULY HAPPY, BUT WE OFTEN PURSUE THE OPPOSITE TO PROVE OUR VALUE.

@smitherystyle

Finding my purpose has been a twenty-year process. Today, I am in my first year of business ownership and am loving it! There have been times when I felt I was off track and burned out. And times when I've done things to help others reach their purpose at the expense of my own happiness. But with every new chapter of my story, I was collecting breadcrumbs to lead me here.

Like so many of you reading this, I found myself balancing a full-time career with the demands of being a parent. In my fifteen-plus years on the corporate treadmill, I often spoke to other women about the challenge of being a working mom. There is a quiet sadness in the era of balancing parenting and full-time work. It is relentless at both ends, and it's often a recipe for burnout, or at least it was for me.

In the summer of 2024, after a career in marketing, I hit the pause button. I took three months of short-term disability leave for burnout. This move shocked a lot of people, because from the outside I looked like I had it all, but in reality, my body and my mind were in a downward spiral. Things needed to change; I needed to take back control.

During this pause I slept in, soaked in time with my girls, worked with a psychologist, read several books, and listened to podcasts. I did the work to finally get to the bottom of my feelings. I took a look at my personal breadcrumbs and wondered, *How did I end up here?*

Two things became crystal clear for me during my leave from work. First, I needed to be in the driver's seat for the remainder of my working life so I'd be able to balance the demands of my personal life. Second, I cared deeply about my work identity and wanted to use my education and experience in whatever my next adventure was going to be. I still had another chapter to write, but instead of it being someone else's story, it was time for it to be mine.

THE IMPORTANCE OF FOLLOWING THE BREADCRUMBS

Getting to where I am today was a process of following my "personal breadcrumbs," the clues that move you toward purpose. They are the things that bring you joy, that you are naturally good at, and that are a group of experiences *unique* to you. Add them up and you may start to more clearly see your path toward purpose and what your next chapter might look like.

 THE CLUES TO YOUR PURPOSE LIE IN THESE VERY PERSONAL AHA MOMENTS.

Here are a few of mine.

I wanted to be a mom but didn't want to stay at home: My mom likes to tell a story about when I was around four years old. I would go to local garage sales and collect Cabbage Patch dolls. I had so many that she put a crib in my bedroom to hold them all! Apparently, I told her I wanted to have lots of kids but that she was going to raise them. This idea foreshadowed my struggle after becoming a mom and still wanting a career. My mom didn't have the same choice, something I always believed was highly unfair. Today, my husband and I work as a team to find a balance that is unique to our family so we both have time for our kids and our careers.

Figure skating fueled my love of fashion: Growing up, my identity was tied to being a competitive figure skater. My parents put me in skating as an outlet for my boundless energy, but I was really drawn to the sport's fashion. For my first competition, at the age of six, I wanted an "all together dress." I always wore skating dresses to practice. I eventually hung up my skates, but I kept my favorite dresses. Maybe one of my daughters will one day wear my early couture fashions.

Recently, I decided to go back on the ice as a member of Trinity synchro adult skating team. I joked in a post on Instagram that I couldn't wait for the spandex and rhinestones. I guess some things never change no matter your age!

Entrepreneurship is in my genes: Some traits are nurture and others are nature. There are highly successful entrepreneurs on both sides of my family, so I'm pretty confident genetics had something to do with my desire to buy a business. After university I told my dad I wanted to start a business instead of working for "the man." As the son of an entrepreneur himself, he told me to "go make mistakes with someone else's money first." I took his advice and landed a corporate job, but I always approached every job with an "owner's mindset." Don't get me wrong, the guaranteed paycheck was pretty addictive, but I didn't find fulfillment in these jobs because I was always dreaming of being my own boss and starting something for myself.

My earliest jobs were in retail, and I loved them: My first jobs in retail taught me about the psychology of sales and the importance of building relationships. I genuinely liked helping others feel confident in their style and I enjoyed building relationships with my clients.

I didn't even consider retail as a career path. It just wasn't appealing with long hours and minimum wage. However, these jobs taught me the foundation of building relationships and the basic mechanics of sales, which would prove to be valuable in both my early career in PR (selling a story) and now in leading Smithery Style where I am building a community, earning their trust, and, at the end of the day, selling confidence through style.

I found working in a small environment more rewarding than working large corporate: During summers of university, I worked for an entrepreneur. I was their sales and marketing manager. My job was soup-to-nuts: I would do calls to book in the clients, work with the website team to get the clients' websites created, coordinate the staffing follow-up, and close the loop asking for reviews.

I thrived in this job because I could really see year-over-year my portfolio grow in value. I had the big responsibility of running a team. I excelled at client relations: I always made sure to make notes about the contacts so that with every client call they felt a connection to me.

I realize now after working in big industries like banking and media where you are just a number that I preferred working for a smaller company where I could see my impact and help drive the business results without needing to gain buy-in or approval. I learned that when I am doing what I do naturally, which is connecting with people, problem solving, and making things happen, I have fun and feel fulfilled.

My pandemic pivot into teaching: The pandemic was a forced pause for me. I didn't go back to CBC after my maternity leave ended with my second child because the government closed daycares, and with two children of daycare age, "social distancing," and no real end in sight, I took on my new role as "head of childcare" in our home. I enjoyed this time with the girls, but something about it being forced was hard to swallow.

Six months into lockdown, I was fortunate to parlay my master's degree in communications management into teaching virtually in higher education. I enjoyed teaching, had glowing reviews, and thrived in the online environment. However, teaching is a real "Girl Friday" gig. You have very little job security and are not paid for anything other than your time in the class. But I learned that I liked operating in an online space, I was good at breaking down complex ideas into digestible lessons, and I honed my public speaking skills. All important tools leading me toward entrepreneurship.

Further, at Smithery Style, one of the things that sets us apart from our competitors is we don't just style our clients, we educate them. We help them discover their body shape and how to dress it. I believe that knowledge is power and you will always remember the person who gave you the key to unlock your problem and that breeds loyalty.

Working for a bank was an unexpected education in purpose-based businesses: After the world returned to normal, so did my career. I took a senior marketing position at CIBC where I was in charge of content marketing for their brand team. This opportunity was a real education in how to use purpose to build cohesion both externally with our clients and internally with employees. CIBC's purpose is To Make Your Ambitions a Reality.

In my role, I worked with the storytelling team to find and tell stories of clients whose ambitions we made real. The banking world has a lot more heart than you might imagine. But three years into this role the tug of wanting to bet on me returned. This time, however, I knew whatever it was had to be deeply connected to my own personal story and purpose.

My struggle with body image became a North Star problem I wanted to solve: Having been in a judged sport that has a lot to do with how your body looks, I have long struggled with being body positive. I remember the day when Mavis Huntley, the founder of Smithery Style, an e-retailer and stylist service that helps busy Canadian women shop for their body shape, came to speak to my mom's group. I was eight months post-partum and was really struggling to get dressed in the morning. This unexpected crisis of style confidence was not something people talked about. I remember Mavis's ability to make me feel as if this was normal and that there was hope for me to enjoy getting dressed again once I learned the rules to my new body.

As women, we undergo many transitions in our lives. For the vast majority of us, this precipitates a change in your body shape. In my case, I'd gone from being an X to being an O. These two shapes have very little style rules in common, so naturally, I was really struggling to get dressed. I slowly rebuilt my wardrobe using my new rules and mostly with items from Smithery because they tag everything that's good for your body shape. It's like a paint-by-numbers way of shopping.

I've always been interested in the "disruptive trends": I am a millennial, and we are a unique generation who have grown up in a post-internet, post-globalized world. I have long been fascinated with what's new and next. My master's thesis was on influencers and how communicators could harness their power well before influencers were mainstream.

The frame of "disruption" was one I had when I was searching to buy a business. I believed that post pandemic there was a growing comfort in the idea that you could order just about anything delivered to your door. E-commerce felt like it really spoke to my generation, so when I had the chance to acquire Smithery Style, I knew the timing and the fit were right for me. I think doorstep delivery of your seasonal wardrobe refresh is an example of a distribution. Instead of being a local boutique, we are a national boutique for Canadian women. Instead of coming to us, we come to you!

WHAT I KNOW NOW THAT I AM WRITING MY OWN PURPOSE STORY

In my newish role as the business owner, I'm able to use all the skills I've acquired over my life. Nothing I did was a waste of time. It was all part of the journey. I have the purpose of helping other women by curating body-positive clothing that normalizes that beauty is not about what size you are but rather how you dress for your shape and reach for things that make you feel comfortable and confident.

We are often told it's people and not things that make us truly happy, but we often pursue the opposite to prove our value. Likewise, my move toward entrepreneurship was not for the money. In fact, writing this today, a year after investing my own life savings into this business, I'm not yet replacing my previous paychecks. However, we are slowly but surely moving the needle toward profitability.

Regardless of compensation at this early stage, business ownership has been transformative in my ability to own my time. Finally, after years of others owning my time, it's exhilarating to decide how long to work, where I want to work, and what projects I am best to work on versus delegate to others. My belief today is that being a mom and being successful in my life's work are not mutually exclusive. They are deeply connected.

I feel the work I do matters to the women I serve. The woman I once was: a busy mom, wife, friend, daughter, employee. I hope I make getting dressed in the morning the easiest part of *her* day. I now know the things that came before were my breadcrumbs helping me discover my purpose, leading me to where I am today.

If you are at a crossroads in your career, I hope you see in my story that you're not alone. Listen to the little voice inside you and follow your breadcrumbs toward your life of purpose.

Chapter FIFTEEN

FIND YOUR SWEET SPOT IN LIFE

To my husband and best friend, Gerry, for your constant support since we were fifteen; to our kids, Anya and Aiden, who have been my inspiration, pride, and joy; and to all the lovely women who inspire, teach, and push me to live with intention, courage, and gratitude. May I bring forth these gifts to the women who need it most.

GLORIA ESGUERRA

From a six-figure career to living a cozy life, Gloria (a.k.a. Jogie) is an immigrant mom who knows a thing or two about reinvention. She came to Canada from the Philippines twenty-five years ago, pregnant and unemployed, and went on to build a strong family, thriving career, and community. Through her own journey, she harnessed the power of sharp analysis and strategy and found her sweet spot in life. Now, as the founder of Analyze This Life, she helps other immigrant women build a life of purpose by embracing their unique paths.

@analyzethislife

THE MORE IN TOUCH AND AWARE WE ARE ABOUT OURSELVES, THE MORE CLARITY AND CONFIDENCE WE EXPERIENCE AS WE MOVE THROUGH LIFE.

@analyzethislife

I can still hear my *lola* ("grandma" in Filipino) telling me: *"Maraot man ang Dai, Maraot man ang Labi."* (Too little or too much is bad; moderation is a better option.) Like Goldilocks, she believed in "just right" conditions. Her strong beliefs and balanced outlook influenced me from an early age.

EARLY LESSONS

When I was only two, I was left in my home country of the Philippines with my maternal grandparents while my parents and older siblings moved to the bustling and busy Quezon City, ten hours away. I was deemed too young to accompany them, so I spent several years with my grandparents in Iriga, only reuniting with my family when I was old enough to join my siblings in school. I remember feeling so alone and sad during those times. I mostly played by myself, often playing house and imagining a happy family. I accompanied my grandfather while he made chocolate from cacao, fed his pigs, or visited his farm. And my grandmother sang me lullabies and told stories of their early family life. At night, I remember staring at my mom's picture before falling asleep, trying to remember her. I missed her the most. Though bittersweet due to my family's absence, these memories taught me my first vital lesson: Families belong together.

I found the transition back into the family fold difficult, as I often felt left behind and struggled to find my place. As the youngest, I wasn't included in conversations. Too young to contribute or share significant experiences, I often kept quiet, observing and listening. I wondered: *Do I even matter?*

I felt lonely, even in the company of my siblings, and I was unable to share these emotions with anybody else. I usually felt disregarded and invisible, except in school. While evaluated as a gifted, fast learner needing special education, I struggled in math with the advanced curriculum. Standing alone in class, unable to answer multiplication flash cards, was not just embarrassing but also deeply terrifying. I often found myself looking out the window, wishing to be outside instead. I constantly fell ill and felt constant dread about school. When I asked my mom if I could quit, she matter-of-factly outlined the alternative: becoming the family maid, which made me quickly reconsider. In third grade, I vowed to do better, determined to overcome challenges and graduate with honors. This instinctive aspiration for better outcomes pushed me to persevere and strategize. Without parental prompting, I applied myself to studying, seizing opportunities to shine and participate in extracurriculars. Each year, my academic standing improved, my leadership was recognized, and I excelled in activities like dance, theater, and journalism.

FINDING CLARITY

Learning to cope and thrive became a pattern I repeated throughout my life. Every setback and obstacle presented opportunities to learn, pivot, and overcome. As the editor-in-chief of our school paper, I was obligated to compete in press conferences, but I quickly recognized that I don't perform well under intense pressure or time constraints. A humbling experience, it taught me to focus on my strengths: putting the school paper together, honing my big-picture vision, and managing details. This was an early lesson in understanding my sweet spot for productivity while maintaining my well-being.

Later, when I was starting out in my advertising career, the constant hustle, networking pressures, moral dilemmas, and long hours made me realize it wasn't a good choice for the future family life I envisioned. I needed to recalibrate my life choices in light of my changing priorities, actively seeking alignment with what truly mattered. I learned this lesson when I watched my mom struggle between keeping the home and family intact while coping with demands from a career that was not her choice. She made do with work that was born out of necessity instead of heartfelt intention. As I grew older, every occasion that made me feel distant from my family also made me realize that I had the capacity and ability to do things differently.

A BIG MOVE FORWARD

Pregnant with my first child and still feeling lost and unfulfilled with work, I moved to Canada twenty-five years ago with my high school sweetheart, whom I'd married the year before. Our decision to move was influenced by my husband's earlier visits to the US. He realized that our dream of being present for our kids while living a life of ease was possible by moving abroad. Since my elder sister had previously moved to Canada, it was easier to embrace the idea of uprooting ourselves and moving to Toronto. We planned to start a family and live a different lifestyle abroad.

Two weeks after receiving our permanent resident visas, my husband and I hastily resigned, packed, and said goodbye to family and friends. It was a deeply vulnerable time with little opportunity to process the profound upheaval. Our elders worried we were abandoning lucrative careers for uncertainty just as our baby was due. My husband left his management role in a big multinational firm, while I left a teaching position at a prominent university after completing my master's degree in communication research. My father was especially upset about the sudden move. There was little time to prepare and get accustomed to this new reality. Indeed, it was the biggest leap of faith of our lives, one we were fortunate enough to take. We held big hopes, trusting we were on the right path to building a healthy family life. This practical philosophy inspired me to seek my sweet spot in this new country rather than blindly climbing someone else's mountaintop.

Early on, my husband and I agreed to prioritize family over career. We both grew up with fathers often absent for work, leaving our mothers to juggle family and career alone. We realized that not having both parents, especially in early childhood years, can take a toll on establishing closeness and family bonding. I felt I hadn't recovered from the early separation and isolation of being left behind. So, determined not to repeat that pattern, we didn't consider leaving our baby behind while establishing our careers. This meant making a deliberate choice for me to initially stay home with our child, a decision enabled by my husband's well-paying job. We understood this was an opportunity not afforded to everyone.

Settling into Canada with a new baby took considerable time and effort. Fortunately, we relied on family, friends, and colleagues for support. While my husband focused on being the sole breadwinner, I took care of our daughter full-time until she was old enough for daycare. This period, while deeply rewarding, also came with its own set of anxieties about my career progression and financial contributions. I restarted my career slowly with part-time retail, then moved to a call center administrative role, and then a contract position in an IT company supporting a cross-border sales team. Each role was a strategic step toward my coveted role. While it was often difficult and unsettling, filled with moments of self-doubt and financial worries, I never lost sight of my early goal to secure work that offered generous compensation, work-from-home flexibility, and enough challenge to keep me engaged and fulfilled. It was a tall order, requiring significant maneuvering and a willingness to start over in many ways, a common experience for immigrants.

FINDING MY SWEET SPOT

After years of dedicated effort, I finally landed the role that truly suited me. My work as a business analyst played to my strengths. I investigated processes, reported findings, and identified improvements that provided leadership with clear insights for informed decisions, boosting employee morale and company revenue. My career progression was intentionally slow, as I prioritized managing a growing family of four with the birth of my son. I wanted to be present for my children while balancing the demanding roles of a working mom and wife. I wanted to spend more time in my sweet spot rather than focus my energies on the pursuit of climbing the corporate ladder. Choosing to spend more time seeking balance—where my values aligned with my daily actions—made it easier to witness and participate in my kids' important growth milestones. This meant breastfeeding both kids for a couple years, being present at early childhood milestones, being easily accessible and flexible to my kids' needs, and, for the most part, avoiding the guilt that often plagues working moms. This wasn't a choice without trade-offs, but it was a deliberate one that allowed me to align my life with my deepest values of keeping my family together and honoring my own needs. In essence, this is my sweet spot.

As my career stabilized, I shifted my focus to our financial health, moving from persistent debt worries to disciplined money management. This requires education and awareness. We adopted new spending habits, implemented expense tracking and frequent reviews, and decided to pay ourselves first through saving and investing. We made each other accountable, discussing big expenses and coordinating decisions as we committed to providing our family a taste of both luxury and frugal living. We did not deprive our kids of learning opportunities (art, music, athletics), and we exposed them to the importance of giving and service. This process became another pillar of our sweet spot—understanding that financial well-being is a priority for stress-free living. Every major decision was deliberated and viewed from the perspective of: Will this benefit our family? Will the kids positively develop from this experience? What is the outcome we want to achieve from this decision? By being intentional and clear from the beginning, we avoided many mistakes that might easily lead to failure. When we do make mistakes, we view them as learning opportunities to improve. We openly discuss what happened and avoid escalating conflicts to an irreparable state. Our family operates as a unit and genuinely enjoys each other's company. We often celebrate and give thanks for the blessings we've enjoyed through the years.

SHARING LESSONS LEARNED

My husband and I spent many years building a comfortable, sweet life in Canada. A life lived in moderation, just like my *lola* used to say. Now that both kids are grown, pursuing careers in dentistry and chiropractic medicine while living healthy and happy lives, I am ready to focus on my next chapter: coaching, mentoring, and entrepreneurship. After helping my kids decide on their sweet spot by trying new things, learning from each experience, and pursuing something they genuinely care about, I felt called to help others do the same. By adopting well-being practices and engaging in community work, I'm using the same principles of self-awareness and intentional growth for this new adventure. It'll require the same skills and intentionality I harnessed in previous iterations. Now called to serve immigrant women, I'm leaning on my own experience and journey as a springboard to create a community of like-minded women focused on building meaningful lives. As I experienced, being an immigrant woman can be lonely and isolating as we navigate life's challenges. But with enough awareness, knowledge, and support, there's nothing we can't accomplish.

The huge amount of courage it takes to leave one's home is only the beginning. It takes grit, resilience, and strong self-belief to build a solid life foundation. This calling demands the same skills of deliberate analysis, strategy, and intentionality that I've honed throughout my life journey. This is why I decided to name my coaching business Analyze This Life. I'm leveraging my analytical skills and experiences to serve and create a community with inspired women—whether navigating immigration, career shifts, family life, or simply seeking more fulfillment—focused on building meaningful lives. My goal is to help women discover and design their version of a sweet life. I call it a "5-Star Life." This concept is inspired by Leonardo da Vinci's model of the "perfect man," an epitome of balance and harmony. My 5-star life framework (5-Star Life: Your Blueprint for Personal Sweet Spot) follows that universal principle while distilling wisdom from other popular frameworks of what constitutes a purposeful life. Just as I was inspired by my family to live a life without regrets, this framework is about intentionally crafting a balanced and harmonious life—your sweet spot—that aligns with your deepest desires and values, regardless of your starting point or unique circumstances.

A 5-STAR FRAMEWORK FOR LIFE

I modeled the 5-star framework after our human body, requiring all parts to be in perfect harmony. Our head represents Health and Well-being—strengthening our mind-body-spirit connection, and being mindful of our environment, lifestyle choices related to play, self-care, habits, and routines. Our hands represent Work and Money (left) and Personal Growth (right). Together, these empower us to manifest our life's purpose. Through continuous learning and application, we reap and sustain the fruits of our labor, building material and intellectual wealth. What keeps us stable and committed to our purpose are our core Relationships and the Community we belong to and serve, represented by our feet. This serves as a strong foundation that keeps us grounded, thriving, and connected to a purpose far beyond ourselves, offering the crucial support system we all need. And at the very center of this framework is Me/You, symbolized by our torso that holds our heart and sustains our life. This covers our different identities and roles, our unique values and beliefs, and the rich tapestry of our lived experiences and memories, all of which lend a distinct quality to our individual lives. This inherent uniqueness means our personal success criteria will always differ from others.

The more in touch and aware we are about ourselves, the more clarity and confidence we experience as we move through life. This is the key to finding your sweet spot. When guided by this framework, one can easily determine which area needs work and improvement.

 THE INTENTION IS TO HAVE ALL AREAS OF OUR LIFE OPERATING AT THEIR HIGHEST LEVEL OF SATISFACTION, YOUR SWEET SPOT, AS EVERYTHING IS INTERCONNECTED, JUST LIKE OUR HUMAN BODY.

By having this framework at the forefront of building your meaningful life, you can navigate any challenge or adversity.

My life journey taught me that with self-awareness, knowledge, and support, transformation is possible. It takes grit, resilience, and self-belief—anchored by that inner understanding of ourselves, as explored through this framework—to build the strong foundation of a 5-star life. This commitment to self-awareness and intentional action, applied through your unique circumstances, is the key to your continuous journey toward your sweet spot.

Chapter
SIXTEEN

CHALLENGES HELP YOU FULFILL YOUR PURPOSE

To my incredible husband, for providing unwavering support as I stepped into the unknown of building a business. To my boys, for teaching me endless lessons and extending grace as I fumble my way through motherhood and business. To every mom who isn't sure she's making an impact—you are—keep up the good work.

KRISTA FRAHM

Krista is a marketing strategist and copywriter who helps practitioners and MedTech companies reach the people who need their solutions most. She brings a decade of experience as a clinical occupational therapist, deeply understanding the industry and client perspectives. Through Krista Frahm Agency, she and her team create effective, ethical sales funnels, email campaigns, and launch strategies.

@kristafrahmagency

IF WE'RE NOT CAREFUL, WE MISS FULFILLING OUR PURPOSE COMPLETELY BECAUSE WE'RE AIMING HIGH AND MOVING FAST INSTEAD OF SEEING WHAT'S IN FRONT OF US.

@kristafrahmagency

What if your purpose isn't big and shiny? What if it's not building an orphanage in a third-world country or standing on a stage motivating millions?

This doesn't make your purpose *any* less meaningful or less worthy of pursuing. In fact, I think far more of us are called to be off the stage, out of the limelight. Rather than one grand purpose and mission to champion, we have multiple micro-purposes that create an effect larger than we realize. This is *just as* important as the person who is speaking to millions.

Just like a tiny pebble creates a ripple effect in still water, your seemingly tiny purpose(s) will ripple and create change in those around you and in the world. One huge rock can create big waves in one area, but some of us have a handful of smaller rocks. And all those little rocks can create ripples in spaces that the big rock's waves may not reach. When you find *your* purpose and *your* meaning in the world, you impact the people who need you the most.

FINDING MEANING

I've always been somewhat of a wallflower. I prefer to work behind the scenes, donate anonymously, and lay the groundwork that sets up other people for success. In high school, I decided to become a physical therapist (PT). I wanted to help people heal so they could continue living their lives and doing the activities they love. I also knew I wanted a "mom job"—something that would allow me to work part-time and be flexible for my future kids.

My very first job as a teen was working with a young boy who had multiple strokes before he was born. I would do activities with him during the day, or I would hold him overnight and comfort him through the seizures that often struck. This behind-the-scenes work allowed his parents to get much-needed rest. His mom is a PT and taught me so much about the brain, rehabilitation, and seeing the person instead of the disability.

Most people saw this boy and assumed he "couldn't"—couldn't understand, couldn't communicate, couldn't grow. But over time, I learned how he communicated his preferences and moods, and when he was just being a silly kid or trying to trick me. It was hard work, not a glamorous job, especially compared to my friends who worked at the mall, but it was impactful. I enjoyed knowing I was making a difference.

I also saw my grandparents struggle with health challenges over the years. Heart failure, Parkinson's, memory loss, addiction, and even suicide. As a teenager, I didn't know how to help, but I saw how devastating chronic pain and the loss of independence were for people of any age. One grandfather even said, "If they take my keys, I'm done." Indicating life without independence wasn't worth living.

These early experiences gave me insights, skills, and compassion that I would need later to fulfill my purpose. Of course, I didn't know that at the time. But do we ever know that life's events and experiences are preparing us to fulfill a greater purpose down the road?

What are you facing right now in your life that may be setting you up to help others later on? What challenges are you facing that will make you the exact right person to help someone else?

WHEN ONE DOOR CLOSES, LOOK FOR AN OPEN ONE

After college, I was set on attending graduate school for physical therapy. I had graduated early, was newly married, and had a plan to fast-track into my career and then start a family. If you're also the type A, planner, perfectionistic type, do you recognize this? If we're not careful, we miss fulfilling our purpose completely because we're aiming high and moving fast instead of seeing what's in front of us.

We moved to Washington State because, according to my deep dive and spreadsheets, it had the best combination of therapy school options, tuition rates, climate, cost of living, and job opportunities for my spouse.

I knew I needed one additional course to apply to PT school. I assumed this would be no big deal since there were three universities in my chosen city. But what I didn't know was that the universities all wanted me to take multiple prerequisites before I could take the course . . . and based on their rotating class schedules, this would take almost two years. As you can guess, I didn't have time for this in my "fast-track plan." Truth be told, we also didn't have the money to pay for that many courses as a part-time student. As much as I clung to that door and tried to keep it open, it was closing.

How many times do we do this in life? We stare at the closed door. Or we find a crowbar to pry it back open, certain that we're meant to go in that direction. Meanwhile, another door is wide open, warm breeze flowing as it invites us to step through if we would only take a breath and look. Eventually, I let the door close, ripped up my PT school application, and searched for a plan B. I hadn't noticed previously, but right next door to the PT program was the occupational therapy (OT) program.

You may not have heard of OT. Most people haven't, or if they have, their understanding is very limited. It's a vast, holistic therapy that leverages creative problem solving to help people engage in activities that are meaningful to them and live life to the fullest.

I didn't even fully understand OT, even though I'd worked in an OT hand therapy clinic as an aide in Colorado. As far as I could tell, it was kind of like PT . . . just for hands. I now know this is a wildly narrow and inaccurate perception, but it was what I needed at the time to convince me that it would be "good enough" if PT school wasn't an option. Not surprisingly, the door to OT school was *wide* open. It's where I was meant to be. I got an in-state tuition waiver, additional scholarships, and was accepted on my first try.

Some of us need the reminder over and over again:

 STOP HOLDING ON TO THINGS THAT AREN'T FOR YOU AND OPEN YOUR HANDS TO RECEIVE WHAT <u>IS</u> MEANT FOR YOU.

Hindsight is 20/20, and I can look back now and say without a doubt that I was meant to be an occupational therapist rather than a physical therapist. I not only learned how to help people heal physically but also emotionally and socially. I learned all about the sensory system, neurodiversity, and how it was possible to make changes to the environment and the task to help people succeed rather than simply trying to change the person.

I see everyone and everything through this lens now. Whether it's a child melting down in an airport bathroom, a ninety-five-year-old man who refuses to stop mowing the lawn, or an employee scared to return to work after an injury has healed. There are holistic, person-centered ways to help these people live full, vibrant lives.

I made it through OT school, clinical rotations, and passed the boards. I was helping people rebuild their lives after strokes, car accidents, heart attacks, and more. I also worked with people during the final weeks of their lives, whether they were 22 or 102, helping them live out their last days with as much dignity and control as possible in a medical facility.

I loved it and felt aligned with my purpose. I was doing the work sixteen-year-old Krista only dreamed of, but that wasn't the only part of her dream I was fulfilling. In the midst of it all, I became a mom as well.

PURPOSE ISN'T JUST ABOUT A CAREER

During my last clinical rotation—still technically a student yet working full-time at the hospital—the smells started to bother me. If you've ever spent time in the intensive care unit, you know that *everything* smells terrible. But when you work there, day in and day out, you build an immunity to it. Unless you're pregnant.

We had assumed it would take a while to start a family. I heard stories of fertility struggles from friends and family, and I understood the statistics, but we were blessed with a pregnancy much quicker than we anticipated; I still needed to finish school and pass the boards, and my husband was in the police academy.

Not my timing, but God's perfect timing, and it opened up the door to a purpose even greater than my career.

Our firstborn is incredible. He's hardworking, wildly intelligent, and compassionate. Although he was overall a happy baby, he was also extremely sensitive. Sounds, lights, touch, foods . . . everything was too much for his little system. He also had a lazy eye, which impacted how his visual system developed in those early years.

A few years later, we had another son. He is creative, artistic, and hilarious. He's strong and healthy now, but he cried constantly as a baby. He would be inconsolable for hours at a time, and we never knew when these bouts would strike until we figured out his food allergies. We lived in fear of the next wave of wailing and didn't trust anyone else to watch him because I was convinced they would shake him.

Becoming a parent wasn't exactly how I'd imagined. I needed every ounce of medical knowledge and advocacy skills I had to get answers and solutions for our kids—for us. Many of my concerns were dismissed. I was told I was over-reacting or that they would grow out of it eventually. Deep in my soul, I knew there were ways I could help them, and I was relentless in looking for answers.

I cut back on my work hours and focused on raising our boys. This allowed me to shape their lives, advocate, and help them develop. It also meant I was able to help others who were also facing challenges because every single difficult thing we faced with our kids has primed me to help someone else who is struggling with something similar.

YOUR PURPOSE SHINES IN THE MICRO-MOMENTS

I've had thousands of conversations with parents to help them better understand what their child is experiencing, how they can best support them, and what resources to seek out. The conversations usually start when they apologize in an exasperated way, tears brimming in their eyes. These conversations happen everywhere . . .

- In airport bathrooms, when the auto-flush toilets are unbearable for sensitive kids.
- At the park, when a child refuses to climb or swing like all the other kids.
- When the doctor tells parents that it's "just colic" and will eventually end.
- In preschool, when the teacher says a child needs to "just try harder."
- When a child is labeled "anxious," but nobody has mentioned their sensory system.

I see their frustration, anxiety, and hopelessness. Conveniently, I have personal experience and a degree that help me help these parents and their kids. This has continued through every stage of my children's development.

We're entering the teen years now and I'm still noticing, asking questions, and mentioning solutions to parents with kids of all ages. Raising kids doesn't get easier over time, it just changes.

YOUR PURPOSE WILL CHANGE OVER TIME— STAY FLEXIBLE

I'm not working clinically as an OT anymore. After a decade of hands-on work with clients, I hung up the isolation gown and started a business in a completely different arena: marketing.

If you told me this even two years before I made the switch, I would've laughed. Being a therapist was my goal and I found deep meaning in the work, but there came a point when I realized I'd lost my passion for it. I sat on the edge of a hospital bed with a wonderful elderly man who was taking a rest break and realized I had zero desire to be there. I knew I had to make a change because I refused to become *that* clinician. We've all met a healthcare provider like that, right?

We were fully homeschooling both kids at this point. Juggling school and managing a home, plus my inconsistent work schedule, were all taking a toll on me, but more importantly, it was negatively affecting our boys. They needed consistency and stability during this post-pandemic season. I saw how other kids were falling apart, and I was dedicated to supporting their mental and emotional health along with providing academic education. If you parented a neurodiverse kid during this time, you know it was no easy task.

I felt like a complete failure for wanting to leave clinical care, but I had to. From a place of burnout, I found copywriting and marketing. I didn't expect this business to have anything to do with my purpose beyond being more available for my kids and family. I simply wanted a way to bring in a little money without having to stop homeschool lessons and run into town when there was a new admission to the hospital.

It didn't take long for me to start writing for other practitioners and see how my work had the potential for a far greater impact in healthcare. We all know the healthcare systems are broken, no matter what country you live in. Practitioners have months-long waitlists for far too short appointments. We don't get the answers we need or the support that can truly help us. But individual practitioners are reinventing service delivery. They're creating courses, programs, and memberships that provide more comprehensive solutions without the red tape found in traditional healthcare. These practitioners are highly educated, specialized, and deliver life-changing results. The problem is, they're not marketers. And many avoid marketing or worry it doesn't feel aligned with their values. This is where I step in and bridge the gap.

I understand healthcare and how practitioners think. I know the system gaps and their educational backgrounds, including the faulty thinking that it plants in their minds around promoting themselves and working outside the lines of healthcare. I provide marketing services, including launch strategy, email marketing, consulting, and more to help practitioners connect with the best-fit clients and make more sales ethically.

I love this work because I get to help fellow practitioners *and* far more patients than I ever would have if I was still treating clinically. It also fits with my personality because I work behind the scenes and lay the groundwork to help someone else achieve great success. You may never know what businesses I support or launches I've had my hand in, which is fine by me.

It allows me to support my family while supporting others. It also gives me the time and space to continue to help friends, family, and complete strangers with my OT knowledge when those teachable moments arise. This is my purpose during this season of life.

Will it change again? Potentially. It's easy to look back and see how things in my life have lined up to allow me to fulfill my purpose along the way, but it's not easy to see when you're in the middle of it.

So, remember to stay curious and open to new paths, especially if you can leverage challenges you've faced and help others. And don't ever, *ever*, minimize the validity of your purpose simply because you're not standing in the spotlight.

Chapter
SEVENTEEN

THE INFLAMMATORY
WORK LIFE

To my parents, Ms. Ashraf Hosseiny and Mr. Reza Boroomand, whose love grounds me; to my son, Elias, whose presence gives life meaning; to my mentors, Dr. Amira Klip and others, whose wisdom shaped my path; to my students, whose curiosity keeps me learning; and to women in leadership, may you embrace audacity as strength and carry forward a legacy of courage, kindness, and impact in navigating the Inflammatory Work Life.

DR. PARASTOO BOROUMAND

Parastoo (Paris) is an award-winning speaker and visionary leader whose career reflects a purpose-driven triad of medical education, humanitarian leadership, and academic pursuit. With a PhD in biochemistry from the University of Toronto and executive training from Harvard Business School, she brings a unique blend of scientific expertise, strategic leadership, and cross-sector experience spanning healthcare, pharma, academia, and nonprofits. She has held multiple director roles across leading medical education agencies, is an adjunct professor at the Temerty Faculty of Medicine, University of Toronto, a 2x best-selling author, founder of House of Boroumand (HoB) Consulting Firm, and serves as the president of the Kindness Foundation of Canada.

LinkedIn @parisboroumand

THE INFLAMMATORY
WORK LIFE: A CALIBRATED
STEADY STATE THAT HARNESSES
URGENCY FOR PROGRESS WHILE
DELIBERATELY GUARDING
AGAINST CHRONIC STRAIN
COSTS IN THE WORKPLACE.

LinkedIn @parisboroumand

INITIATION: INTRODUCTION

The lens through which we see the world is ever evolving, and what a privilege it is to shift, adapt, and let new experiences redirect us. I learned this lesson early in my undergraduate studies at the University of Toronto. At the time, I was enrolled in physical and mathematical sciences, convinced I would understand the world by modeling it with equations. But after struggling through a linear algebra exam (or maybe a few), I began to question whether I had chosen the right path.

Up to that point, I had never taken a single biology or chemistry course, not even in high school. Yet the following semester, I registered for both, determined to broaden my perspective. I vividly remember first encountering the macrophage in a textbook: a cell whose morphology intrigued me even before I understood its function. Later, I learned that macrophages are remarkable cells of the immune system, capable of adopting diverse phenotypes to preserve tissue balance, yet, under certain conditions, are also capable of unleashing chaos and disease. Both protectors and instigators, healers and disruptors. That paradox struck me deeply. I didn't know it then, but this was the beginning of a journey that would eventually lead me to complete a PhD in biochemistry, studying the obesity-induced immunometabolic activation of myeloid cells. Put more simply, the inflammatory wiring of the macrophage lineage through weight gain.

Inflammation, I came to understand, is far more complex than its poor reputation suggests. It is often framed as purely destructive, yet in its acute form it is one of the body's most essential defenses: a precisely orchestrated surge that mobilizes immune cells to neutralize pathogens, clear damaged tissue, and initiate repair to restore homeostasis. Without acute inflammatory responses, even a minor infection could prove life-threatening. Chronic inflammation, however, is when the defense system fails to switch off, like an alarm that never stops ringing, the ongoing inflammatory activation begins to damage the very tissues it was meant to protect. Over time, this persistent activation scars organs, disrupts normal processes, and sets the stage for the onset of various disorders. Homeostasis is the steady state through which the body regulates its internal environment. It was first articulated by Claude Bernard and later expanded by Walter B. Cannon in *The Wisdom of the Body* (1932). Cannon described it as the "maintenance of steady states in the body and the physiological processes through which they are regulated," a concept now foundational to modern physiology.

So, why am I giving you a science lesson here? Well, I never imagined I would draw on those findings outside the laboratory. Yet across academia, the nonprofit sector, and the corporate world of medical education, I began to see striking parallels between the biology of inflammation and the dynamics of leadership, particularly for women in healthcare. Acute bursts of urgency, when focused and finite, can galvanize progress and sharpen performance. But urgency without resolution, the chronic "always on" state of unrelenting demands, drains creativity, erodes well-being, and weakens organizational vitality, much as chronic inflammation depletes the body. In much the same way, we must find a homeostasis of productivity in the workplace, a steady state of output that never outruns our vitality.

One of my earliest director roles made this parallel especially clear. At first, the pressure was invigorating. Urgency lit a fire, and my team thrived; focused, sharp, and determined to deliver. But as weeks stretched into months and the intensity refused to relent, what once fueled us began to corrode our strength. Fatigue crept in, creativity dulled, and even small obstacles became insurmountable. We often said:

if everything is urgent, then nothing is urgent; and, in effect, nothing got the attention it deserved. These reflections brought me to what I've defined as the Inflammatory Work Life: a calibrated steady state that harnesses urgency for progress while deliberately guarding against chronic strain costs in the workplace.

This realization reshaped my understanding of success. It is not defined by constant combustion but by a dynamic equilibrium: knowing when to ignite and when to recover, when to surge and when to sustain. This is the lens through which I invite you to read this chapter. Each section parallels a stage of inflammation—initiation, recognition, amplification, mediation, resolution, and return to homeostasis—so that the science of the body becomes a road map for the science of leadership.

RECOGNITION: THE HEALTHCARE LEADERSHIP GENDER GAP

Recognition is the body's first act: innate sensors detect danger and set the response in motion. Organizations work the same way. We have to recognize patterns of experience, including the different paths many women navigate and what registers as threat or unmet need, before we can improve the system.

Women form the backbone of healthcare: nurses, physicians, researchers, educators, program directors, and frontline caregivers. According to the World Health Organization, women make up nearly two-thirds of the global health and social care workforce. Yet, they are starkly underrepresented in healthcare leadership. The *Women in Healthcare Leadership* 2019 review found that women hold roughly 30 percent of executive roles and fewer than 15 percent of CEO positions in healthcare. This persists despite decades of incoming talent and clear evidence that women leaders strengthen innovation, ethics, culture, and patient outcomes.[1-3] The common "pipeline problem" explanation doesn't reflect the reality of this gender authority gap in practice. These barriers are often less about talent and more about perception of authority, both as expertise (credentials, knowledge, experience) and as leadership (being respected in charge). It is also felt in how confidence is frequently mistaken for competence, allowing men's overconfidence to be rewarded with opportunities, while women feel pressure to over-prepare simply to earn credibility. Unequal pay, thin sponsorship, biased promotion practices, and rigid expectations around caregiving create bottlenecks where momentum stalls.

I've felt this in subtle ways in boardrooms. I was often one of few women, aware that my comments carried the weight of representation. In professional networks, I watched men be casually ushered to mentors and sponsors who later opened doors—without navigating the burden of the male gaze. Stretch assignments that build visibility (turnarounds, high-stake launches, keynote slots) were often allocated through informal circles to men. While women were steered toward "office housework" (committees, notes, onboarding, patient-satisfaction fixes): valuable work, but not promotion-making. Evaluations policed tone; what read as "decisive" in men became "too direct" in women. Caregiving collided with after-hours meetings and inflexible on-call expectations. None of these alone ends a career, but together they widen the gap the higher you climb on the corporate ladder.

I was fortunate to have women leaders who advocated for equity and opened doors I might never have reached alone. So, I know what it looks like when inequities are actively challenged. The costs are not only personal, but they are also systemic, an unresolved imbalance between contribution and representation. Time and time again, there are evidence that organizations with diverse leadership are more innovative,

1. Muraya KW, et al. BMJ Glob Health. 2025;10(2):e014945.; 2. Tsugawa Y, et al. JAMA Intern Med. 2017;177(2):206–213.; 3. American Medical Women's Association (AMWA). 2023.

resilient, and better at solving complex problems.[4-7] In healthcare, where decisions affect patient safety, resources, and health equity, the price of homogeneity is especially high. Lack of diversity narrows the lens through which problems are defined and solutions imagined. If healthcare hopes to heal at scale, its leadership must reflect the diversity of those who deliver care every day.

AMPLIFICATION: STRENGTHS AND STRESSES UNIQUE TO WOMEN LEADERS

In biology, amplification is when an initial signal becomes a coordinated cascade. Work has its own amplifiers: board and regulatory timelines, quality metrics, staffing shortages, always-on channels, and the invisible load of emotional labor and "glue work" (the coordination that keeps teams moving but rarely earns credit). Tuned well, these forces concentrate focus and momentum; left uncalibrated, they normalize constant intensity and turn sprints into the baseline.

When women step into leadership, strengths like initiative, empathy, collaboration, and resilience can be converted into unwritten expectations of "she'll take the hardest project, smooth the conflict, and stay available after hours." At their best, those strengths build trust and spark innovation. Under bias and continual urgency, they get overextended: empathy becomes constant caretaking of the team, collaboration becomes unseen coordination, and resilience becomes silent endurance. Over time, I've learned that answering every late-night ping and filling every gap trains others to expect it. What I called reliability became permanent availability; resilience hardened into rigidity, and the more I delivered, the less visible the effort became. Lois Frankel's *Nice Girls Don't Get the Corner Office* captures this paradox: behaviors encouraged in girlhood such as accommodation, conflict

---

4. Lorenzo R, et al. Boston Consulting Group (BCG); 2018.; 5. Woolley AW, et al. Science. 2010;330:686–688.; 6. Hunt V, et al. McKinsey & Company; 2018.; 7. Zenger J, et al. Harv Bus Rev. 2019.

avoidance, and perfectionism, can sabotage women in leadership positions.[8] The organization harvests the labor; the recognition migrates elsewhere.

 THE AIM ISN'T TO MUTE OUR STRENGTHS BUT TO ARCHITECT CONTROL AROUND THEM.

Pair empathy with shared coverage and clear response norms so care doesn't cannibalize capacity. Pair collaboration with visible ownership through decisions documented and roles defined, so "glue work" converts to recognized contribution. Pair resilience with identified escalation thresholds, channeling heat into structural fixes instead of private overwork. This way, healthy amplification mobilizes without consuming strengths that scale, momentum that serves the mission, and leaders whose energy remains both visible and renewable.

MEDIATION: ORCHESTRATING THE STRESS RESPONSE IN LEADERSHIP

In the body, mediation is orchestration: inflammatory mediators widen vessels, increase permeability, recruit immune cells, and steer cascades toward defense or repair. Their job is to turn signals up when danger persists and down before the response becomes self-destructive. Healthcare leadership demands the same orchestration. The stakes are performance, equity, and representation. When I first stepped into leadership, I felt both the authority of the role and the weight of bias: resolve conflict without seeming "too aggressive," stay steady under pressure without being labeled "too soft"; experiences unfamiliar to my male peers. The balance of mediation then felt like a gendered craft that women disproportionately practiced to keep systems functional.

Contrarily, conflict is neutral; unmanaged it festers, managed well it

---

8. Frankel LO. *Nice Girls Don't Get the Corner Office.* Rev ed. New York (NY): Business Plus; 2014.

transforms. "Orchestrating conflict," as Ronald Heifetz coined it, can be leveraged to hold tension long enough for adaptive learning, protecting dissenting voices, and pacing distress so it stays productive. I practiced this once, and many thereafter, at a heated advisory board meeting deadlocked between specialists and administrators. Rather than rush to closure, I acknowledged the discomfort, invited opposing voices to contribute, then moved to solutions. What could have derailed became a productive turning point. The dissent exposed blind spots, and the proposed solution carried more weight because everyone felt heard. Here, I held the heat long enough for learning to take place without letting it burn the room.

However, empowerment without boundaries can backfire. Autonomy energizes, but it can also fuel overwork and burnout, as seen with many nurses. Effective mediation adds a second dimension of psychological hardiness, the habit of viewing stress as challenge which buffers burnout and helps women leaders build cultures where pressure drives adaptation, not collapse. An important adapting point for me has been realizing that mediation is direction-less. My job isn't only to support my team, it's also to influence up and across so we fix the system. Practically, that means making care structural: clarifying decision rights; defining escalation thresholds so "crisis" has a shared meaning; building predictable coverage that doesn't depend on heroics; and setting norms that treat recovery as part of the job. In short, mediation isn't soothing conflict or absorbing stress in silence, it's redesigning the conditions that create it.

RESOLUTION: CULTIVATING A HEALTHY ORGANIZATIONAL (IMMUNE) SYSTEM

Resolution is when inflammation subsides, pro-resolving mediators restore balance, and healing begins. Without it, the defensive response lingers into dysfunction. Organizations face the same inflection point. What separates cultures that heal from those that corrode is whether leaders design for resolution. Think of culture as the organizational immune system. When healthy, it senses problems early, responds in proportion, remembers what worked, restores balance, and prevents relapse. In my experience, teams with strong speak-up norms surface issues fast, treat mistakes as data, and invite diverse perspectives that act as antibodies against blind spots. By contrast, brittle cultures mimic unresolved inflammation: dissent goes quiet, trust erodes, and the system attacks itself.

For many women leaders, the labor of resolution is expected and invisible. The fix isn't to work harder, it's to make recovery structural so resolution doesn't depend on heroics. Here's what that looked like in my practice. We created early-warning channels, brief safety huddles, and open office hours, so weak signals surfaced before they became crises. We built short after-action reviews into the week, capturing "learning opportunities" so experience became organizational memory. We set stop rules and cool-down windows such that every surge had a defined end, and leaders modeled shutting the alarm off. Workload was load-balanced with predictable coverage, and we treated time off as capacity, not a perk. Finally, we ran relapse checks such as scans for bias, burnout drivers, and corrosive habits to keep gains from slipping away.

This way, resolution was cultivated, not assumed. For healthcare leaders, it means designing cultures where recovery is valued as much as urgency, where diversity is treated as an adaptive strength, and where equity is woven into the immune memory of the system. It also means advocating that the labor of resolution (listening, repairing, and rebalancing) is recognized as leadership, not dismissed as emotional caretaking. Mediated poorly, cultures resemble chronic inflammation, consuming people and their performance. Resolved wisely, they become organizational immune systems: adaptive, resilient, and capable of healing while moving forward.

RETURN TO HOMEOSTASIS: A NEW MODEL FOR LEADERSHIP

In the body, healing completes when the system returns to homeostasis. In leadership, that return blends repair, regeneration, and balance: we restore capacity, rebuild capability, and reset the conditions that keep energy renewable. It begins where resilience and empathy meet, adapting under pressure while keeping people connected. Acknowledging that the clearest lessons often result from setbacks: a faltering project, a stretch role, a brush with burnout that force to recalibrate. Acknowledging these realities builds trust and makes recovery a shared skill. Regenerative leadership doesn't mean doing less, it means leading differently. Designing cultures where productivity rides on sustainability, urgency is reserved for true crises, and human energy is treated as a core asset. This way, ambition becomes fuel rather than fire.

The operating system is a dynamic leadership equilibrium: coupling "where we're going" with "how we get there" and constantly balancing the needs of the organization, the people in it, and the community it serves. Under strain, imbalance shows up as predictable stress behaviors. The fix is to calibrate growing competence deliberately, tethering confidence to evidence rather than bravado, and aligning control so authority matches accountability. When competence, confidence, and control line up, communication widens, resources flow to priority work, and teams can downshift cleanly back to homeostasis.

To conclude, I invite you to build your own Inflammatory Work Life where you steward the flame and the fuel: recognize early, amplify wisely, mediate well, resolve deliberately, and return to homeostasis. Lead with a dynamic equilibrium of the work, the people, and the enterprise. Then watch results endure, teams rise, and the culture become self-repairing. This is Your Life on Fire.

Chapter EIGHTEEN

WHAT LIGHTS YOU UP?

To all the amazing entrepreneurs who have supported me along the way; you've kept me going. Thank you!

CARI BRUNTON

As an event strategist, speaker trainer, and marketing director, Cari is always focused on helping her clients grow their businesses. She brings her creative passions to helping entrepreneurs streamline getting clients so it's an easier and faster process that lets them focus on the parts of business they love. Cari's clients add six figures to their revenue, build simple and repeatable marketing and sales systems, and host events that turn attendees into clients.

@redbucketevents

THERE ARE A LOT OF CHALLENGES IN LIFE THAT CAN TAKE YOUR PASSION AWAY. SOMETIMES YOUR PASSION CHANGES. SOMETIMES IT GETS REALLY QUIET AND WAITS FOR YOU TO FIND IT AGAIN.

@redbucketevents

I've found most of my passions over the years by falling into them.

My father has been an entrepreneur for my entire life. His business has gone through several iterations, and for the most part, he's been incredibly successful. During the good years, it was easy to be happy: We took vacations and participated in a variety of extracurriculars. When new obstacles popped up, my parents had enough money to pay for help. But during the lean years, things were a lot harder. The stress from not making enough sales spread from my father to the rest of the family. My parents fought more, worried more, and enjoyed life less.

I've seen exactly what happens to families when business is slow or even stagnant. It doesn't just hurt the entrepreneur, it ripples out to their partner and kids. I seem to collect entrepreneurs everywhere I go—my brother is one, my partner is one, and I've made a lot of friends who are ones too. So, when it came time to choose the best audience to help with events and speaking, I've become most passionate about helping entrepreneurs create consistency in their sales so they can live their lives exactly how they want to, without the stress. It's not easy to find your purpose, so if someone is brave enough to not only find theirs but to use it to create a business and help people, I want to help them make sales and marketing as easy and as fun as possible.

FINDING YOUR SPARK IN SOMETHING NEW

I was working as the marketing and content coordinator for a charity in Niagara Falls when my boss announced, "You're going to plan our Easter fundraiser this year." She left me to figure it out. I loved it. The creativity, the planning, the process . . . it was like a sandbox made for my skills and talents. It invigorated me. The true beauty of events is that you build something that people come to and enjoy. It's an exhilarating feeling.

After that contract was done, I wasn't ready to give up on events, so I spent a year getting a post-graduate certificate in event management. Thanks to the entrepreneurship class, which in no way prepared me to be an entrepreneur, I started to really consider the idea of running my own business. I liked the idea of being able to choose events that really excited me.

I got a full-time event management job, and in a momentary lapse of sanity, I envisioned running corporate events with big budgets, better hours, and cutting-edge trends. I was thinking about fun retreats and employee engagement, but instead I organized fundraising events for small charities, which meant small budgets and minimal staff. I spent so much time at the dollar store that I knew how to find things better than the employees. During a lull, I was laid off from my job, which seemed like a great time to pursue my own business. More accurately, I was sitting on my couch and saying I was doing things while achieving nothing. Thank god for unemployment benefits.

A few months later, my previous employer offered me my job back. I countered by offering to make them a client and they agreed, becoming my first client of Red Bucket Events. I had a part-time job waitressing to try and even out the income roller coaster I was experiencing every month.

That was 2019. At the start of 2020, I had picked up a few more clients, received a business grant to improve my website and marketing, and felt like a rocket about to take off. Then COVID-19 hit. It was a terrible time to be in the live event business, particularly in Canada, when everything, including my business, came to a screeching standstill. I felt completely unfulfilled, nothing feeling as purposeful as planning and executing events. I was depressed and listless. I spent as little money as possible but focused my efforts into networking. Even my waitressing job didn't exist anymore, and while I didn't miss coming home with screaming feet and smelling distinctly of pasta and butter, I did miss the cash.

BE FLEXIBLE WHEN THINGS CHANGE

People started asking me about webinars, which skyrocketed as soon as live events stopped. I handled their event marketing, and as I listened to these speakers, I was struck by the impression that many of them weren't great. So, I watched these speakers. I could see how their movements were distracting instead of enhancing, how they missed opportunities to connect with the audience, and how they highlighted the wrong things about their services.

I started public speaking when I was four (yes, I'm aware that's slightly freakish) and felt fired up with the idea to combine my marketing, sales, and event planning with my knowledge of public speaking to help others sell their services. When I hosted my first webinar, I was incredibly excited. I had roughly thirty people in attendance, and I let out all my passion as I was speaking. Here was something I could love while events were gone. The audience was engaged, and I got plenty of compliments when I was finished.

But nobody bought a single thing. I felt like a complete moron. Here I had been so confident that all my training and experience blended together perfectly so that I could do this. And the idea of teaching was so thrilling. So, I licked my wounds and decided to dig deeper. I spent time studying speaking to sell, sales psychology, and other presentation techniques to understand what I did wrong. And when I was ready, I hosted another webinar—then filled my calendar with sales appointments.

I knew I had to teach other entrepreneurs how to do this. I've watched so many entrepreneurs struggle with marketing and sales, and it lights me up to simplify it for them. I was able to help my clients create streamlined marketing systems that stopped the stress of feeling like being on a content-making hamster wheel. When you know how to speak to sell, every podcast, networking group, or summit becomes a chance to fill your calendar without feeling like a sleazy salesperson. One of my favorite moments was when a leadership coach worked with me, gave her first talk, and got a client from that talk, which she had been convinced she wouldn't be able to do. Those moments fueled me.

BUILD OR REBUILD AS NECESSARY

Rebuilding was a slow process and it felt like starting over, helping people learn to trust me again with a different expertise.

 SUCCESS ISN'T A STRAIGHT LINE, AND MINE WAS ABOUT AS SQUIGGLY AS IT CAN BE.

I reached a point where I had tens of thousands of dollars in debt and developed anxious hives from worrying. I'd held my debt as my stressful little secret for so long that I finally broke down and told my partner, Mike. He took it better than I expected. I asked my family for help, who took it exactly as badly as I expected, but they did help me on the condition I went back to work full-time. My part-time clients weren't providing a consistent income, so I bought a briefcase and turned myself into Corporate Barbie. Tragically, my shoulders are way too broad to rock a pantsuit.

I sobbed my eyes out just thinking about looking for a job. The idea of working where I had little control, minimal influence, and often no chances to use both my creativity and my logistical skills burned my heart. I constantly felt shame, surrounded by my own failures, and like I was completely giving up my own dreams. I was devastated.

I got really lucky and found an event planning job that was 90 percent remote, only needing me in person on prep days and for events.

Flex hours were standard for the whole office, and no one cared when I worked as long as I averaged seven hours a day. The staff were a wonderful and helpful group who provided fantastic training and support. It was such a nice change, getting paid to learn new things after years of paying to learn. And I was still able to take on my own clients and continue with my weekly business group for mindset work, strategy, and training. Without that program, I suspect I would have lost all focus and just stopped working on my business altogether. My coach really kept me moving forward and cemented in me that you should always have a coach to pull you out of the mud.

But there were still large blocks of time when I'd miss those meetings and do nothing in Red Bucket but small client work. I didn't market myself, nourish my relationships, or do anything that would grow my business. I occasionally took speaking gigs that popped up, but I didn't actively search for them.

Whenever I got even the smallest chance to teach another entrepreneur and help grow their business, it felt like my heart resumed beating and my inner light was shining. But then I'd go back to the daily grind of my day job. Having no say over what clients we took on and what events we focused on was very difficult for me. Input is one of my biggest values, but I didn't have much of that at this job.

WHEN DISAPPOINTMENT LEADS TO SHAME

I particularly didn't love that many of the clients wanted to host the same events the same way every year and weren't interested in innovation. I tried to focus on the positive—I was getting a lot of experience running large conferences—but I didn't feel like my work had any real impact.

For the first year or so of working my "day job," I was too embarrassed to tell any of my entrepreneur friends that I had gone back to corporate. I dropped out of networking groups because I was afraid of how they would view me if they knew my situation. How dare I claim to be able to help other entrepreneurs with growing their businesses when I hadn't managed to keep myself out of debt and disorder? I was convinced that I had a scarlet "C" for corporate sellout pinned on my chest for everyone to mock.

Letting go of that shame started when I had to tell a few clients about my work schedule. I was surprised when they had no reaction. I kept waiting for their judgment, but it never came. And they still wanted to work with me despite my schedule constraints. After a few of these experiences, it finally dawned on me that every entrepreneur understands doing whatever you have to do to keep the dream alive. Take out a loan? Sure. Get a day job? Will do. Ask for help? Absolutely.

The black cloud of embarrassment started to break up inside me and a few new larger clients came my way. I was making an exciting amount of money. Not quite enough that I felt I was ready to leave my day job, but it was significantly closer. And I could feel my inner light sparking back up, growing and becoming more visible.

Spring and fall are the height of conference season, and I knew I was headed into a particularly busy spring. The company was working on more events than the last year with fewer staff, and my work for Red Bucket Events was more than double what it was in 2024. I did my best to pace my way through it, remembering I was fairly burned out at the end of the previous spring, but stress was winning at every turn. I was eating poorly, gaining weight, sleeping horrendously, and exercise didn't even occur to me. Mike was supportive, but he had a day job and an entrepreneurial adventure of his own, so my not having mental space for taking initiative of any kind around the house was slowly weighing on him.

But as I counted down the days until June, I realized that it wasn't just the past two months of overwhelm I'd been feeling. I'd let so many of the things that brought me pleasure slide. I prefer my nails to be painted at all times but hadn't done them since October. I couldn't remember the last time I'd baked something or tried a new recipe. I'd skipped over Christmas baking entirely, which is normally a sacred tradition for me.

I was barely even playing with my cats, and my two gorgeous fluffballs usually bring me so much joy. My passion for life had eroded by trying to cling to my passion for my business and to make enough money to quickly pay off my debt.

FIGHTING BURNOUT

I went to the CEO and explained that while I enjoyed working for their company, I was really struggling. I asked if part-time was an option. The CEO came back with an offer to become my client instead, buying chunks of hours as they needed them and using me as a trusted contractor.

The joy and relief I felt was palpable. I couldn't have dreamed up a better option. I was a little scared about losing the consistent paycheck, but I was ready to feel like I was living my life again instead of just trying to survive it. After my last official day with the company, my two biggest clients each had events in June, so I had projects to throw myself into. As much as I promised myself I'd take a break after that and slow down, my body wanted to take that break immediately. I made it through but dropped balls I shouldn't have. So, I'm trying to focus on what I've learned as I go forward.

As I write this, I'm still feeling the struggle of burnout, but I'm trying to go slow but steady. I'm adding speaking events to my calendar, and clients are calling. My passion for life is coming back too. My nails are currently an energetic purple, I baked Nutella pinwheels last week, I played with my cats this morning, and my relationship with Mike is back in a good place.

There are a lot of challenges in life that can take your passion away. Sometimes your passion changes. Sometimes it gets really quiet and waits for you to find it again. But keep your eye on it. Do what you need to do and take care of it and yourself. It's your flame that keeps clients coming back for and puts a smile on your face every day. Helping entrepreneurs thrive is what lights me up, and I am absolutely loving it.

1

Chapter NINETEEN

THE QUIET EXIT

For Filipe and Isabel, my heart's greatest joy; for my dad, sister, brother, and Virginia and Lidia, every page carries a piece of you. None of this would exist without your love and presence in my life.

CRISTINA BALAU-HODGINS

Cristina is an HR executive, speaker, and advocate. Curious, adventurous, and fiercely committed, she blends leadership acumen with a love of travel, history, and sociology to inspire others, help them find their voice, and champion causes for abuse victims and individuals with disabilities.

@thri_ebeyondlabels

SUPPORT DOESN'T MEAN TELLING SOMEONE WHAT TO DO. IT MEANS SHOWING THEM THEY'RE NOT ALONE, EVEN WHEN THEY'RE NOT READY TO ACT.

@thri_ebeyondlabels

Leaving wasn't brave—it was necessary. Staying meant fear, control, and danger I could no longer ignore.

I didn't wake up one day suddenly ready to go. It was a slow, painful realization that staying was costing me everything: my peace, my sense of identity, and my ability to trust myself. The fear wasn't just about what he might do next. It was the constant pressure, the emotional manipulation, the way he used our son to keep me in line.

He kept us isolated. Controlled our movements. Made sure we didn't build connections outside the family. To the outside world, there was nothing to see—no obvious signs, no cries for help. Only his parents and siblings knew what was really happening. Everyone else saw a quiet family, not the control and fear that defined our daily life.

And it wasn't just me being affected. My son was living in it too. He was required to carry the secrets, to pretend everything was fine. He couldn't grow the way a child should—with joy, safety, and freedom. I saw the weight on him, even when he didn't speak about it or couldn't express his feelings. I knew I had to remove him from that environment. I couldn't let him think that this was normal, that the dynamic we lived in was anything other than pure control.

To survive, I learned to minimize what was happening. I told myself it wasn't that bad. That things would get better. That he would change. I clung to hope because the truth was too painful to face. Years later, my therapist explained that this is common among survivors. The pain is so overwhelming, we compartmentalize. We separate the worst parts from our daily reality just to keep functioning.

I was also ashamed. Deeply ashamed. My perception of abuse had always been tied to addiction, something dramatic and obvious. I thought abuse looked a certain way, and that people who stayed were somehow at fault. So, when it happened to me, without those markers, I didn't know how to name it. I didn't know how to ask for help. I blamed myself. I thought it was my responsibility to make it work.

But the truth is, I was breaking. Slowly. Quietly. And I knew if I didn't leave, I'd lose myself completely—and I'd lose the chance to protect my son from the same damage.

Leaving wasn't a clean escape. It was messy, terrifying, and full of guilt. But it was the first step toward reclaiming our lives. I didn't leave because I was strong, I left because I had no other choice.

And that choice saved us, the three of us.

THE DAY I LEFT

I didn't and still don't have any family in Canada, so we had nowhere else to go. But I wasn't completely alone. Even though he kept us isolated—controlling where we went, who we saw—we still attended the congregation. That's where I met someone who would become a dear friend, an ally. In that moment, having someone who saw me, who believed me, made all the difference.

I had been thinking of leaving for months. Quietly building the courage. Trying to figure out how I could do it, how I could protect my son, how we could survive. Then I found out I was expecting my second child. Fear overcame me. I wondered if leaving was even possible now. How was I going to do this pregnant, with a child already depending on me? Faith gave me the strength to keep moving forward.

But things had become so unbearable I couldn't wait any longer. Things were not going to change. And I knew that once I left, I would never go back, because if I did, it would only get worse.

I'M READY

I remember the moment with absolute clarity. I called my friend and said, "I'm ready. It has to be today, and it has to be in the next couple hours—he just left the house." She didn't hesitate or ask questions. She simply said, "I'll be there."

She didn't have her car with her, so she called a trusted friend. That's when they became my Batman and Robin, my heroes in plain clothes. They arrived quickly. No panic, just purpose. They helped me pack: clothes, my son's toys and books. While I was stuffing bags, she was on the phone with shelters, trying to find a place for us. She even called the school to let them know we were coming to pick up my son. Every detail was handled with care and urgency. Words will never be enough to describe the love I have for Batman and Robin. They didn't just help me leave, they helped me believe I could.

Before we went to the shelter, I sat my son down and explained what was happening. He was calm, silent, and concerned . . . but not for himself. "Who is going to make Dad dinner?"

That question broke something in me. It showed me just how deeply he had been conditioned to prioritize someone else's needs over his own. Even in a moment of upheaval in which all that he ever knew was unraveling, his instinct was to care for the person who had caused us both so much pain.

But we left. We chose ourselves. And that was the beginning.

THE FIRST WALK

The day after arriving at the shelter, I left with my son to pick up some essentials. I was apprehensive. I knew he was out looking for us. Every step outside felt like a risk.

We were walking hand in hand when my son looked up at me and said, "Mom, I like walking with you."

That moment stopped me. It had been years since I had walked alone with my son—without tension, without fear. I felt a quiet, growing strength that told me this was going to be the first of many walks. Just the two of us.

The time at the shelter taught me a lot—not just about survival, but about clarity. It showed me what I didn't want for my future, and what I refused to accept for my children. I met incredible, courageous women and their children. Women who, like me, had believed they couldn't survive without their partner. That they couldn't provide for their children or maintain the life they had been accustomed to.

I learned that abuse doesn't discriminate. It exists in every layer of society. It doesn't care about income, education, culture, or background. It hides behind closed doors, behind smiles, behind silence, and it gains strength in its secrecy.

I also saw the heartbreak of cycles. Women who arrived, left, and returned a week or so later. Each of us was on our own journey, moving at our own pace. Holding our own stories close to the chest, there was no judgment—only understanding and quiet solidarity.

I reached out to my family. I told them I had left my marriage, and why. I was worried about how they'd respond. I should not have been; they were supportive. Encouraging. Loving.

If I can share one thing with anyone in an abusive relationship, it's trust that your loved ones will be there for you.

 ABUSE THRIVES IN THE SHADOWS OF SHAME AND FEAR. BUT WHEN WE EXPOSE IT, IT LOSES ITS POWER.

Their love, understanding, and unwavering support has carried me through the years. It reminded me that I wasn't alone, that I had always been loved. That I was still part of something bigger than the pain.

With guidance from the shelter, I found a lawyer and began what would become years of court battles. It wasn't easy, but it was necessary.

If I wanted to build security for myself and my children, I had to be willing to fight for it. This was also the time I discovered the power of community. I was slowly finding a small, mighty group of people who wanted to help. People who showed up, listened, and offered what they could. It was real and it mattered.

REBUILDING

Rebuilding was not easy. I had to find an apartment, a job, and a way to support myself and my children. There were weeks we barely made it—stretching every dollar, every ounce of energy. But I was confident. Not because I had all the answers but because I had decided to believe and draw strength from God and myself.

There was a voice inside me, quiet but persistent, that said, *I will prove them wrong*. The ones who said I couldn't do it. The ones who thought I'd go back. Maybe that wasn't the healthiest motivation, but it pushed me forward when everything felt heavy. It gave me fuel when I had nothing else.

Through the years, I built a stable home and a career. A life. Not perfect, but safe. Not easy, but ours. My children had a place to grow, to laugh, to heal. And I had a place to breathe. I was granted sole custody, which gave me a sense of security. But he still had visiting rights. That part was complicated. It brought its own challenges, its own emotional weight. But I focused on what I could control—our home, our routines, our peace. Every step I took was a step away from fear and toward freedom. And while the journey was long, I never stopped walking.

I hope my story gives even one woman, one person, the inspiration to tap into the strength already inside them. To leave. To give themselves the right to feel safe. To discover what it feels like to be loved. Because love doesn't equal fear. Love doesn't mean pain. There is no right time. There is only your time. And it begins the moment you choose yourself.

THE RIPPLES

Spousal abuse doesn't just affect the partners, it touches those close to us, our children. It shapes how they see the world, how they understand love, safety, and trust. Children absorb everything. Even when we think we're shielding them from the worst, they feel tension. They hear the silence. They notice the fear and become hypervigilant. And over time, it begins to color their view of relationships, of themselves, of what's "normal."

I saw it in my children. In their quietness. In their questions. In the way they watched me, as if trying to measure whether we were safe yet. It broke my heart each time I had to send them to their weekly visits, at first supervised, especially when my daughter was still a baby. But it also strengthened my resolve.

Our healing didn't happen overnight. It came in small moments. In bedtime stories. In shared meals. In walks where my son held my hand and shared his feelings openly. It came in the rebuilding of trust and in the quiet assurance that we were safe.

NO LABELS ATTACHED

As we settled into our new lives, I was adamant—I didn't want to become another statistic. I didn't want my children to be penalized for what we had been through. That meant making difficult choices and sacrifices. Housing came first. A good school district was nonnegotiable. I wanted them to have opportunities to thrive, not just survive.

Only a handful of people knew our situation, and that was by design. I didn't want the stigma to follow us. I didn't want assumptions made about my children's abilities or mine. So, I was simply a divorced, single mom. No additional labels attached.

But the truth is, I was still holding on to shame. Still carrying my own paradigms about what it meant to be a survivor. I didn't want pity. I didn't want judgment. I just wanted a chance to rebuild without being defined by what had happened.

As my healing journey continued, something began to shift. I became more confident in my purpose. I started to understand that silence, while protective, could also be isolating. I knew that at some point, I might need to share my story with someone I trusted, or with someone who needed to hear it. Because if I wanted to be an ally to those still in abusive situations, I had to be willing to speak. To offer hope. To show that it's possible to leave. To rebuild. To thrive beyond labels.

HOW TO BE THERE

When someone is in an abusive relationship, our instinct is often to fix it. To say, "You need to leave." But what we don't always understand is that leaving isn't just a decision, it's a process. One built on fear, survival, conditioning, and often shame. Support doesn't mean telling someone what to do. It means showing them they're not alone, even when they're not ready to act.

I want to go back and share something truly special. As I mentioned, we used to attend our congregation. One day, the wife of a couple we knew approached me quietly and said, "I'm here for you when you need." I was taken aback. She later told me my eyes grew wide, and I immediately looked around to see if he had heard. That reaction said everything. She repeated herself gently: "I can see something is not right. Don't worry—I won't say anything."

I didn't respond. I just nodded and moved along. But I never forgot it. Each time she saw me, she quietly reassured me. No pressure. No judgment. Just presence. From the first time she reached out to the day I finally called her and said, "I'm ready," four years had passed. She never gave up on me. She never told me what to do. She was just there—a reminder that I wasn't invisible. That I wasn't alone.

Later, when I was about to go into labor, she was the one I called. And once again, I said, "It's time." And once again, she replied, "We'll be there." Batman and Robin, my heroes, laughing all the way into the delivery room with me, supporting me, telling me, "You got this."

So, if you want to be an ally, here's what I ask: Don't give up. Don't demand. Don't try to fix. Just let them know—with a smile, a nod, a quiet word—that you've got them. Whenever that day comes. I will never forget the ones who waited years for me, with love, not pressure.

As I reflect on that chapter of my life, I know my journey is only beginning. My voice grows stronger each day. I use it as much as possible to help others—because if sharing my experience helps even one person feel less alone, less afraid, more seen, then it's worth every moment of discomfort. Just as I moved through fear and silence all those years ago, I continue to move forward now with purpose. This voice, once buried under shame and survival, is now a lifeline. And I will keep speaking. For her. For them. For me.

Chapter
TWENTY

LIVE YOUR MISSION
EVERY DAY

To Julia and Alex, may you never lose your spark. As your Poppy used to say, "You gotta do what you love, kid!"

LIANNE KIM

Lianne is a renowned business mentor with over twenty years of sales and marketing experience. She founded the Mamas & Co. community in 2014 with the aim of helping women create wild success on their own terms. Lianne is also an award-winning public speaker, 3x best-selling author, celebrated podcaster, and the creative force behind MamaCon®. Over the last decade, she has helped thousands of women make great money doing what they love.

@liannekimcoach

EVERY DAY WE HAVE THE OPPORTUNITY TO LIVE OUR MISSION IN LITTLE AND BIG WAYS. WE DON'T HAVE TO WAIT FOR SOMEONE TO GIVE US A PERMISSION SLIP TO TAKE ACTION ON WHAT WE BELIEVE IS OUR GREATER LIFE'S PURPOSE.

@liannekimcoach

Over the past decade, I have had the immense pleasure of coaching many women to greatness. Along my journey of self-discovery and self-mastery, I came to the conclusion that my life's purpose is to help others grow, succeed, and feel amazing.

For a long time, I believed the only way to live one's mission was to throw our whole selves into it. For example, by taking our passions and our purpose and turning them into some form of career or business through which we could make a meaningful impact and be well paid in return.

THE MANY PATHS TO FINDING YOUR PURPOSE

But I've since come to the realization that living one's mission doesn't work like this at all.

I NOW DEEPLY APPRECIATE THERE ARE MANY PATHS TO FINDING AND LIVING OUR PURPOSE. AND THERE ARE MANY DIFFERENT WAYS WE CAN EXPERIENCE THAT SENSE OF CONNECTEDNESS TO OUR MISSION, NOT JUST IN OUR WORK LIFE BUT IN ALL ASPECTS OF OUR EXISTENCE.

Not just in the big earth-shattering milestones but in the little moments as well.

I could tell you hundreds of stories of women whose lives have been changed because of the work I do. I am a very experienced coach and have helped so many women accomplish amazing milestones, such as starting and growing successful businesses, catapulting from near poverty to wealth, and creating more time freedom than they ever thought possible. It's been such a humbling and deeply fulfilling decade of transformational work.

RECOGNIZE SIGNIFICANT PATTERNS IN YOUR LIFE

But when I really stop to look at my whole life, not just the last decade but my entire journey, I see some very pronounced patterns and trends. Many similar moments where I leaned into my greater gifts to help change someone for the better. Not just in my career but in lots of other areas as well. Allow me to share a few stories with you to highlight this. In some cases, individual's names have been changed to protect their privacy.

One of my first memories of playing the role of coach was when I was in my twenties. I worked at a local travel company and was surrounded by many like-minded young people. One woman in particular stood out to me as needing some guidance. Marnie was disorganized and had a lot going on in her personal life, which led to her often leaving her house at the last minute and showing up late and in a tizzy most mornings. Because of her poor time management, she couldn't take transit because it would have taken too long. Instead, she paid for expensive taxis multiple times a week, which started to add up!

Marnie is about five years younger than I am, and I became a sort of big sister figure to her. Over time, she confided in me about her messy life and her dismal finances. That wasn't a surprise to me; she was spending about thirty dollars a day on cab rides.

I discretely took Marnie aside and explained to her that while I was no expert when it came to finances, I knew a few best practices and offered to sit down with her and share them. We met up at a local coffee shop and chatted for a little over an hour. I talked to her about the importance of saving a portion of her paycheck and explained what a registered retirement savings plan was. She had no idea that was even a thing!

In her defense, she was raised by a single mom (whom she still lived with because she couldn't afford her own place), and everyone in her life was living paycheck to paycheck. She was following the example of those around her, but she knew she had to make a change or else she'd never experience financial empowerment. I gave her a few pointers about saving, investing, and budgeting.

From the outside, this encounter might have just looked like two women having coffee. But in actuality, something quite profound was taking place. I was sharing wisdom that had the potential to change her life.

Let's play this out. If she took my advice, Marnie would end up becoming a better saver. And if she continued on that path, she might have invested those funds and started earning interest. And if she continued diligently saving and monitoring those investments, she might have been able to afford her own home one day. Possibly travel, maybe retire early. These things would all have a profound impact in her overall lived experience.

So, what seemed like a very insignificant thing at the time actually had the potential to make a monumental impact on her life's trajectory. I gave her the gift of a small dose of financial empowerment, and in return, Marnie gave me the gift of getting to share my passion for helping people grow and succeed.

I left that job a few years later and sadly, we lost touch, so I will never know if she became the financially responsible, affluent woman she longed to be. But that's not the point of the story. The point is that she now had the *potential* to be!

TAKING MEANINGFUL STEPS

When I look at the last decade of my career as a coach and mentor, there are so many women whose lives have been completely altered as a result of me uncovering and leaning into my passions and purpose. But one who stands out the most is Veronica. She was a gifted designer and had been running her part-time business for about a year while also working for a major company. While she was very good at design, she needed help with the business side of things. She was working herself ragged by wearing all the hats, and she recognized something needed to shift.

She deeply craved a wildly successful business, but she wasn't sure of the next steps. She approached me within my first year of running my coaching business. Once our work began, I could see she was charging way too little for her services, and she was starting to feel the onset of burnout. We worked together for over a year on setting up her business in a way that would allow her to thrive both personally and professionally.

First, we worked on highly tactical details. We adjusted her packages and prices and spent significant time working on her marketing and messaging. It was important the right people could see her work in the right light.

But most of our coaching sessions were spent on her mental game. We spent hours working on her money mindset and self-worth so she could truly feel confident charging her clients what she deserved. As we moved through this work, it turned out her issues around charging her worth sprung from some very deeply ingrained patterns and issues from her childhood.

Not only was it impacting her work, she was also feeling it in her personal life. She confessed that between her day job and her business (primarily evenings and weekends), she rarely saw her family. She felt deeply disconnected from her spouse and it was taking a toll on their marriage.

One day, I could feel that her tension and anxiety were building. I asked a seemingly innocent question and she erupted. "I don't know!

Okay?! I know I should know the answer, but I just don't, so stop asking!" Then she burst into tears. I held space for her as she sobbed for several minutes. She was clearly working through some major issues.

I had triggered Veronica without even realizing it, and I felt awful. But my own mentor reminded me that when we are triggered emotionally, it can be a beautiful catalyst for change. So, I stayed the course and continued to guide her.

Veronica continued to work with me for over a year, slowly and steadily getting closer to her goals. By this time, she desperately wanted to quit her day job because she realized it was holding her back from achieving success in her business. She worked on her mindset, continued refining her strategy, and kept taking one step after the next. Even when things felt hard, even when she was approaching burnout, she never gave up.

I'll never forget the day when Veronica called me in disbelief. "Lianne, I did it! I just passed the six-figure mark! I've made $100,000 in my business in the past twelve months. I can't believe it!"

She was in shock, but I was not. I always believed it was possible for her. It was not long after she messaged me that she finally had the consistency and courage to leave her day job and pursue her dreams full-time. This had a tremendous impact on her family life, her love life, and her physical and mental health. She had more time freedom, which brought her a sense of peace and joy. Being able to go all in on her dreams was truly a life-changing experience for her.

Since then, I've helped countless women quit their jobs and replace their former salaries with their own self-generated income, but Veronica was the first, and I will never forget her. I'm pleased to report that after nearly a decade, Veronica's business is thriving and she has made a name for herself in her industry. She went from making small, inconsistent revenue to being a successful entrepreneur in charge of her worth and her power. In fact, she's likely generated over a million dollars in revenue at this point. She is a true thought leader and now hosts inspirational women's events. She's created more time freedom, a more aligned schedule that works for her family, and she recently reported that she feels more grounded and fulfilled than ever. Every day I live my mission through my work with women like Veronica, and I am so honored to get to do so.

SMALL LESSONS EQUAL BIG PAYOFFS

Another more personal example of how I live my mission was a moment I shared with my two tween children: Julia, 13, and Alexander, 11. Several months ago, our city experienced a very large snowstorm. Overnight, Torontonians had over three feet of snow on their front lawns. My area was particularly impacted. Because of our narrow streets, we are often the last part of the city to be plowed, so the snow was piling up everywhere.

My husband and I set to work shoveling our own driveway, and we asked our kids to help. After helping for a few minutes, they realized what exhausting work it was and demanded to be paid for their efforts.

"I won't pay you," I said, "but I will help you sell your services to other people. Maybe some of our neighbors could use the help. I bet they'd be happy to pay you!"

Within a few minutes, we had a little business on our hands! The kids would go door-to-door and promote their services. They asked if I would ring the doorbell and speak to the homeowners for them, but I told them learning to sell was part of running a business. So, I gave them a little script, a few pointers, and sent them on their way.

Before long, they had their first customers; however, they quickly realized that the five dollars per driveway they were charging was not adequate for the amount of work involved and the amount of time it was taking. So, we discussed options for them to increase their prices. As the day progressed, their confidence in themselves increased. They built up the courage to ask for ten dollars per driveway or five dollars per kid.

Most neighbors felt this was more than fair, and many paid over asking or tipped generously.

After about two and a half hours of this, they came home exhausted but rich! They had made eighty-five dollars between the two of them, and they couldn't believe it. They split their funds equally and began discussing plans for their next business venture.

On the outset, this might look like any ordinary day for our family. But look a little closer and you'll see my mission in action. I was actually guiding my kids toward success by arming them with some very empowering hands-on business experience. First, they learned how to spot an opportunity and seize it, a crucial skill for any entrepreneur! Next, they learned about pricing and pitching their services. They also learned a powerful lesson in handling rejection. If someone said no, they answered, "Oh well, thanks anyway!" and moved on. They also learned the power of teamwork: the importance of sharing the load and working together to get things done efficiently.

I'm telling you, they probably learned more that day than most people learn in an entire MBA program. Okay, I'm exaggerating for effect here, of course, but hopefully you see my point.

Every day we have the opportunity to live our mission in little and big ways. We don't have to wait for someone to give us a permission slip to take action on what we believe is our greater life's purpose. We can begin right now, exactly as we are.

WHAT LIGHTS YOU UP?

What is one thing you could do in the next twenty-four hours that would get you feeling more aligned with your life's purpose? What's something you have to offer that could make an impact on someone you know? Is there someone in your world who already sees you as a mentor figure, and could you offer guidance to them?

Is there a book, podcast, or video series dedicated to the thing you are most passionate about? Perhaps start by doing some learning and getting in the mindset of someone who does this for a living.

If you've enjoyed these questions, I encourage you to pick up a copy of my first book, *Building a Joyful Business*, where you will find an entire chapter dedicated to this kind of self-reflection. It is designed to help you create space to gain clarity on what your own life's purpose is. Whether you own a business or not, it's an extremely helpful resource.

Not everyone is going to have the capability or the means to just quit their job to start a business around their calling. But anyone can pick up a book. Anyone can start to dream. Anyone, regardless of their life situation, can start to lean into their inkling to make a contribution.

I invite you to continue to explore this subject because I know that doing so will have a profound impact on your life, which, in turn, will once again help me live my own mission. Yay!

Continue to reflect on what areas feel meaningful to you. Continue to align yourself with other mission-driven people. Make time and space for regularly living your purpose, not just now and then, but every single day. And even if you are not able to live a life on fire right now, know you're able to light the match and spark that flame.

At fEMPOWER Publications,
we don't just publish books—we amplify movements.

We support thought leaders, visionary storytellers, and creative entrepreneurs
in transforming their ideas into powerful nonfiction books, journals, workbooks,
affirmation decks, and personal growth tools that leave lasting impact.

Our mission is to help our authors protect their soul's work, expand HER
platform beyond the page, and turn HER message into a timeless legacy.

www.fempower.pub | @fempower.pub 📷

www.ingramcontent.com/pod-product-compliance
Lightning Source LLC
Chambersburg PA
CBHW051302120626
46547CB00015B/2054